MY INDIAN REMINISCENCES

MY INDIAN REMINISCENCES

BY

DR. PAUL DEUSSEN
Professor at the University of Kiel

Translated By A. King

GYAN

Published by

Gyan Publishing House
5, Ansari Road
Daryaganj, New Delhi-110002
Phone: 011-47034999, 9811692060
E-mail: books@gyanbooks.com

Distribution Network
gyanbooks.com
India, USA, Canada, UK, Australia, France

ISBN : 978-81-212-3793-2 (PB)

2nd Impression 2020

Printed at: Gyan Press, Delhi.

My Indian Reminiscences
Author: Dr. Paul Deussen

MY INDIAN REMINISCENCES

BY

Dr. PAUL DEUSSEN

Professor at the University of Kiel

TRANSLATED BY A. KING

G. A. NATESAN & CO.
SUNKURAMA CHETTY STREET
MADRAS

CONTENTS.

PUBLISHERS' NOTE.

This is an English translation of Dr. Deussen's "Indian Reminiscences" written in German sometime ago. In the winter of 1892-93, the famous Sanskrit Professor and his wife travelled in India under exceptionally favourable circumstances. Dr. Deussen had notes of introduction from his renowned friend, the late Prof. Max Muller and other well-known Oriental scholars to various officials of rank, officers and others in this country and this gained him access to the hospitable circles of Anglo-Indians in high position. To Indian society of all rank and position Dr. Deussen and his wife had the freest access. His knowledge of Sanskrit, the study of which had been so to speak his "daily bread" for the twenty years previous to his trip was of immense service to him. It easily enabled him to converse in that language not only with eminent personages like the Maharajah of Benares but with Professors, "numerous private scholars, holy men, and ascetics to a surprising extent." And in the villages which he passed through he found the Pandits and Priests opening their hearts to him in the sacred language of their scriptures. Dr. Deussen's scholarly study of Indian Philosophy had enabled him to "enter the spirit of the Upanishads and the Vedânta based upon them" and the profound knowledge of the German Professor of the Vedânta "contributed greatly to break down the barrier that had hitherto separated the European from the Indian." No wonder that the Indian, who came across the learned Doctor "with astonishment, contemplated on the foreigner who was more at home in their sacred writings than they themselves." Hence it was that he "got a deeper insight into the life of the natives than a European usually gets." Dr. Deussen's account of his tour throughout India, his description of its principal cities, its shrines, pilgrimages and its many holy spots, its leading men of various communities and classes afford much interesting reading. The language in which he describes the customs, ceremonies, manners, traits and traditions of the Indian people—not withstanding the shortness of his stay in India—shows his profound admiration and love for the land which to use his own words "had for years become a kind of spiritual mother-country" to him. In the famous lecture which Dr. Deussen delivered before the Bombay Branch of the Asiatic Society on the eve of his departure from India he discoursed eloquently on the Philosophy of the Vedânta and wound it up by the significant criticism:—"And so the Vedânta, in its unfalsified form, is the strongest support of pure morality, is the greatest consolation in the sufferings of life and death—Indians, keep to it." How thoroughly Dr. Deussen and his wife enjoyed their tour in India and how reluctantly they left our shores will be gathered from the following touching lines of their *Farewell to India*:

> O, sun of India, what have we committed,
> *That we must leave thee and thy children now,*
> Thy giant-trees, thy flowers, so well befitted
> To thy blue heaven's never-frowning brow?
>
> And you, our Indian friends, whose hearty feeling
> Deep sympathy with you has fast obtained—
> From Ceylon to Peshawar aud Darjiling,
> Are you now lost to us, so soon as gained?

The publishers desire to take this opportunity to thank Dr. Deussen for permitting them to present to numerous readers—Indian and English—an account of his Indian reminiscences which is sure to be welcome to them.

FAREWELL TO INDIA.

O, sun of India, what have we committed,
That we must leave thee and thy children now,
Thy giant-trees, thy flowers, so well befitted
To thy blue heaven's never-frowning brow?

And you, our Indian friends, whose hearty feeling
Deep sympathy with you has fast obtained—
From Ceylon to Peshawar and Darjiling,
Are you now lost to us, so soon as gained?

Farewell! Now Space and Time, in separating
Our bodies, will create a cruel wall;
Until forgetful darkness over-shading,
Like Himalayan fog, bedims you all.

Did we but dream of your brown lovely faces,
Of your dark eyes, and gently touching hands?
Was it a dream, that left such tender traces,
Accompanying us to foreign lands?

O, yes, a dream *is all* that we are living,
And India be a dream in this great dream;
A dream, repose and recreation giving,
Under a paler heaven's fainter beam.

But what are Time and Space, whose rough intrusion,
Will separate what is so near allied!
Are they not taught to be a mere illusion?
May we not be against them fortified?

O, yes, this thought shall be our consolation,
When we are severed soon by land and sea!
Your sun and ours in one! no separation!
Keep friendship, friends, let it eternal be.

COLOMBO,
17th March, 1893.

P. D.
M. D.

CHAPTER I.

INTRODUCTORY.

IN RECORDING my impressions of my trip to India in the winter of 1892-93, and thus presenting them to the public, I have yielded to the wishes of my friends, partly because, notwithstanding the shortness of my stay in India, I was enabled, being favoured by circumstances, to get a deeper insight into the life of the natives than a European usually gets; partly too because my opinion of Indian life and manners differs widely from that universally accepted, more particularly because, unlike most other people, I have not viewed the Indian land and people through the eyes and interests of the English, nor am I in the habit of kneeling before the golden calf of success, and prone to under-rate a weaker cause merely because victory does not chance to be upon its side.

When at last I saw my way to realize the dream of years, to give up my professorial work for half a year, and hasten, in the company of my wife, to the land which for years had become to me a kind of spiritual mother-country, I was not altogether unprepared for what Fate was pleased to accord me. The traveller in India requires a knowledge of three languages: English to communicate with people of culture, Hindostani in his intercourse with natives, and Sanscrit to speak to the Pandits—the Indian learned scholars, who, as a rule, are entirely ignorant of and have a horror for English. My wife and I were both thoroughly conversant with English, having frequently resided in England. It being almost impossible to get lessons in Hindostani in Germany, we could not begin to learn it until we started on our journey; but we got to know enough during our stay in India to be able to get on with the natives without the assistance of a servant. With regard to Sanscrit, the study of it had been, so to speak, my daily bread for the twenty years previous to my trip, so that I cherished the hope that I might be able, after some practice in the country itself, not only to speak it, but—which is far more difficult—to be able to understand Sanscrit when rapidly spoken, or coloured with dialect. This hope proved to be no vain one. Familiarity with Sanscrit is far the best introduction to the higher native classes, as a rule entirely closed to the average European. Not only do the scholars—in particular the native professors of Sanscrit at the Indian universities—speak Sanscrit with great elegance, not only do the students understand its use as well as the European student of classical philology understands Latin, but the numerous private scholars, holy men, ascetics, to a surprising extent, speak and write Sanscrit with great ease. I have conversed for hours, for instance, with the Maharaja of Benares in Sanscrit; manufacturers and merchants, if they do not speak, at least understand it ; in every little village, my first enquiry was for some one who spoke Sanscrit, whereupon someone or other presented himself, who generally ended by becoming my guide, not infrequently my friend. Frequently I yielded to the request of the natives and gave them an address. This I of course did in English, but I was nearly always asked to repeat what I had said in Sanscrit for those who had not been able to follow my English address. After this had been done, a discussion usually followed, some using English, some Sanscrit, others Hindi, the general import of which I could usually catch, as pure Hindi differs from Sanscrit in little more than the suppression of the flexional endings. In this way every Hindu understands about as much of Sanscrit as an Italian does of Latin, more especially as in Hindostani proper the written characters are the same. You may even meet with a smattering of Sanscrit among the servants and lower classes. A letter to Benares with nothing but an address in Sanscrit will be delivered by any postman without the smallest difficulty. Many Indians seem to think that it is the same all the world over, for among the numerous Sanscrit letters which still reach me from time to time, there was one I remember on which, in addition to all the extravagant compli-mentary titles, my very name was written in Sanscrit characters, in its Sanscritized form of *Devasena*—the place of abode was wanting, and yet, to the honour of our post be it said, it safely reached my hands after having first made its way to Leipzig, where the address was deciphered.

What was to be of still greater use to me in India than the knowledge of the ancient and sacred language of the land, was the fact that I had happened to have spent the best energies of a number of years in entering into the spirit of the Upanishads and the Vedanta based upon them. If, generally speaking, the Veda for the Indian corresponds to what the Bible is for us, the concluding chapters of the single Vedas, termed Upanishads, correspond in contents and tendency to the New Testament; and just as the Christian dogmatics are built up on the New Testament the religious and philosophical system of the Vedanta is built up on the Upanishads, which, in my opinion, must be accounted the best that metaphysical contemplation has produced among mankind in the course of the world's history of thought. At all events the Vedanta is still as of yore the fundament of all higher spiritual life in India. While the lower classes are content to worship idols, every Hindu, in proportion to his capacity for thought, becomes a believer in the Vedanta, in one or other of its various phases, and looks upon all the gods, the worship of whom he leaves to his family. solely as symbols of the *one* Atman penetrating the world and embodied in every man. The exact knowledge and corresponding appreciation of this doctrine on our part contributed greatly to break down the barrier that had hitherto separated the European from the Indian: with astonishment they contemplated the foreigner who was more at home in their sacred writings than they themselves, and with delight they listened to the explanation of how in the Kantian philosophy Europe possesses a doctrine most closely allied to that of the Vedanta, and possessing the scientific fundament the latter wants.

We had, however, no dearth of mere outside introductions to all parts of India. By a happy chance, in September 1892, just before we started for India, the Ninth Oriental Congress had been held in London. There and in Oxford, where we were for several days the guests of Max Muller, it was easy to get a number of introductions from scholars, officials of rank, officers, and so on, who had all spent years of their lives in India. We made use of the greater part of these, and in this way gained access to the hospitable circles of Englishmen in high positions in India, indeed to an extent surpassing our requirements. To be sure these letters of introduction would rather have hindered than facilitated any familiarity with the natives, which we most desired. But here an acquaintance we had made some time before with two Indians was to be of the greatest importance for us, and to bring us into touch with hundreds of others in the country itself. Three years before I had attended the Oriental Congress at Stockholm and Christiania and had made the acquaintance of two Indians there, H. H. Dhruva, late judge in Baroda, and Mansukhlal Nazar, a merchant, who, with two brothers, Atmaram and Utsavlal, owns an important business in Bombay. A fourth brother, Beharilal, was then still at school. In Stockholm, I had invited Dhruva and Mansukhlal to come and see me on their way through Berlin, where I at that time resided; they came, and had since repeatedly written to me and sent me Indian papers. I had kept putting off acknowledging receipt of these missives, until at last I was able to send them a card to say I hoped to land at Bombay with my wife on November 7th. These relations were to be of the very greatest importance for us.

CHAPTER II.

FROM MARSEILLES TO BOMBAY.

ANY ONE INTENDING travelling to India, particularly in autumn, when a swarm of tourists wend their way thither, will do well, by payment of half the fare, to secure a passage three months in advance on one of the various English, French, Italian, North German or Austrian steamship lines. It may be noted that the larboard cabins are to be preferred to the starboard ones, because cooler, as for the same reason the cabins on the upper deck are preferable to lower deck ones, more especially as the port-holes of the latter are so near the surface of the sea that they require to be closed at the least threatening of rough weather.

We had missed the best season for reserving our cabins, and when we began enquiring about passages in London in Fenchurch Street and vicinity, where the offices of the various international lines are to be found, we could at first meet with nothing suitable. The cabins on the P. & O. boats were booked up to the middle of November; this line carries the English mail and is looked upon as the safest, besides taking no steerage, but only first and second class passengers. The Company's biggest and newest boat, the *Himalaya*, advertised to leave for Bombay on October 15th as an extra sailing was, to our great regret, booked up to her last cabin. The name and size of the ship, the idea of occupying entirely new cabins, as well as all that was expected of this new ship made the *Himalaya* appear doubly desirable to us, so when a cabin, being countermanded, happened to be offered, we decided after some hesitation upon taking it, in spite of its being second class, on the lower deck, and the starboard side. We took return tickets, available for six months, *via* Marseilles Bombay out, and home *via* Colombo-Brindisi. With regard to the heat which we anticipated, we comforted ourselves with the thought that, after leaving Suez, we should be able to sleep on deck; the somewhat inferior table was of no importance to us, as even the first-class table on the P. & O. boats has no very great name, and the prospect of spending a fortnight with business men, subalterns, missionaries and so on, instead of with the more elegant tourists, was not without a certain charm. It was a considerable saving too; instead of £80, the price of the first class return ticket, the second class only cost us £50 a head. We had our heavy luggage put on board the *Himalaya* in London, and left it to make the voyage round Gibralter through the stormy Atlantic alone, while we bade a last farewell to our dear ones in Germany, spent a delightfully refreshing day in Geneva with my friend Oltramare, my oldest pupil in philosophy and Sanscrit, to speed on *via* Lyons to Marseilles where we completed our outfit by investing in a very useful deck-chair and two cork sun-helmets.

The latter are quite superfluous on the voyage, but cannot be dispensed with without risk from the moment of landing at Bombay. We went on board the *Himalaya* at Marseilles at 4 p. m. on October 22nd, 1892.

There is no confusion like that which prevails on a big ocean steamer the last hour before she sails. Coaling is going on, luggage being shipped and unshipped; the cook and his assistants are busy receiving huge baskets containing fowls or vegetables; the sailors are handling cables and tackle; the stewards are up to the ears in work, directing to their cabins the new arrivals, who, with their multifarious hand-baggage, obstruct each other's way, while tradesmen and pedlars over-run the ship, offering fruit, jewelry, photographs, and all kinds of rubbish for sale. At length calm begins to reassert itself; traders, and those who have come to see friends off have to leave the ship, the last to leave being the Company's Agent and the postman laden with the letters of the eleventh hour; the steam-whistle gives vent to its last shrieks, the mighty screw begins to turn, first slowly, then with ever-increasing speed, we leave the harbour and are soon on the open sea the coast gradually fading away into the evening twilight behind us.

We proved to have acted wisely in joining the steamer at Marseilles instead of going aboard in London, for the cutting North wind which had accompanied us beyond Geneva as *bise*, to travel on with us to

Marseilles as *mistral*, had raged in the Atlantic as a storm, in which the *Rumania*, a steamer leaving London together with the *Himalaya*, and also on its way to India, had suffered shipwreck. The wind however now calmed down, the waves, which had been pretty stormy when we left the French coast, became smoother, and from that moment till we reached Bombay we had the smoothest and finest of seas. Next morning, Sunday, October 23rd, when I climbed up three stairs from our tiny cabin to the deck to breathe in deep draughts of the pure bracing sea air, I saw the long coast-line of Sardinia on our right, while on the left the sun was gilding Corsica's lofty mountain peaks. The strength of the southern sun already began to make itself felt here, and when towards noon, after Divine Service, I had sat for some time in the sun, with a light hat, I felt so giddy that I determined to look upon this as a warning and not again to expose myself to the sun without proper protection. Next morning in the early dawn on the right Messina with her lighthouse hailed me, a lighthouse I had visited but one year before, without having cherished the hope of seeing it again so soon, nor with such brilliant prospects for the immediate future. The lights of Reggio on the left reminded me of a scanty and hasty meal and of a following long night spent in the train, in the course of which, about 1 A. M., though half asleep, I had heard the station of Cotrone, properly Kroton, called out, the celebrated nursery of Pythagorism. Now all that had no further charm for us, nor were we even huffed to find that Etna had veiled its head in dense clouds. The year before, from Taormina, we had had a splendid bright view of its mighty snow-fields, with the smoke rising in delicate wreaths from its crater.

Sicily's coast was quickly lost to view; the sea became more resplendent in colour, the sun blazed down in greater glory from the dark blue sky above; at last, by no means to our dissatisfaction, it sank in the western waves, and when we saw it rise again next morning from the glowing purple bed of the East, the south coast of Crete, with its splendid mountains was already on the left. The *Himalaya* seemed to be realising our best expectations, and some people had already begun to prophesy that our voyage to India would be a record one—but there's many a slip, as the proverb says. Towards noon, while Crete was still on our left, and on our right a little island, presumably Clauda, where St. Paul's ship, after having left Crete contrary to the Apostle's advice, tried in vain to land (Acts XXVII, 16) something perfectly unexpected befell us—the engines, to whose regular beat day and night we had already become inured by custom, suddenly stopped short, and an alarming stillness followed. General excitement seized on all the passengers, all sorts of conjectures were rife, nobody was able to state anything positive, for nothing was to be got out of the ship's officers, whose duty in such cases is to keep silence. So much at all events was clear, there must be some weighty reason for the unwelcome halt; the *Himalaya*, one of her officers had told me, consumed 110 tons of coal a day, making, with coal at 30s. a ton, £160 a day, so that every delay was costly. At length, after five hours' hammering in the engine-rooms we continued our route, though at reduced speed, so that we took about thirty hours before late in the evening we cast anchor in Port Said, where, instead of clear sea-water we got a dirty kind of liquid for our baths next morning. We lay at anchor here till noon, detained by repairs, looking across at the very middling hotel in which we had once spent a night three years before, and viewing from the deck the busy streets and harbour, without being able to leave the ship, nor for that matter were we boarded by any one—as we had been declared in quarantine, having just come from Marseilles, where cholera was rumoured to be lurking. The only creatures that broke the ban and inflicted themselves upon us as most unwelcome fellow-travellers were a large number of flies, which did not entirely disappear until we got into the Indian Ocean. At last, about 1 P. M., we left Port Said and steamed into the Suez Canal, Asia on our left, Africa on our right, a flat desert on either hand as far as the eye can reach, and between the canal, occasionally widening to an inland lake, but in general a narrow water-channel, double the ship's breadth; overhead the cloudless Egyptian sky, around us the warm, dry desert air, its transparency lending to all objects the most vivid of colours—those were the chief impressions of our passage through the Canal, which went on all night, taking about nineteen hours, as we sailed dead slow in compliance with the regulations, and had to stop at least half a dozen times to let other vessels pass; on account of the prevailing currents the ship has to be moored to the shore at each halt. The next morning Suez lay before us, with lofty mountains in the west behind it, all bathed in a wonderful rosy dawn. To be sure the whole district is arid, if we except the verdantly green banks of the outlet of the sweet-water canal at Suez. After a short stop only we went into the Red Sea; on the left we could gaze all afternoon on the rugged mountains of the peninsula of Sinai, until, its southern point once passed, the sea widens, and for three days all land is lost to sight, with the exception of a few scattered islets. The prevailing great heat makes every one sensible of the fact that the voyage lies across a sea sandwiched between two vast desert continents. Immediately on leaving Suez the ship's officers abandon their dark uniforms and appear in white, an example everyone makes haste to follow. During the meals in the dining-saloon the punkah is kept constantly in motion; it would be almost impossible to take one's meals without the punkah; even at the Sunday services it creaks a dull monotonous accompaniment to the clergyman's voice. It was perfectly impossible to stand the heat in the cabins—a few minutes sufficed to put one in a state of violent perspiration, with inevitably dire results to a fresh collar. Although doors, windows, and port-holes were kept wide open, sleep was out of the question in the cabins; at last I lay down on the floor, using the hard threshold of the open door as a pillow, and when even this failed to bring the desired repose we determined to overcome the resistance of the lazy and invariably prevaricating stewards and gave strict orders to have our bedding taken on deck the following night. This proceeding, despite its inconveniences, was soon followed by all the others and adhered to till the end of the voyage. At 10 P. M., when Mrs. Shakespeare, (an officer's wife with three pretty daughters) had risen from the piano that stood on deck, and when the waltzing couples had separated and a certain quiet was restored, the stewards could be seen panting upstairs from the various cabins with mattresses and pillows; a barricade of deck-chairs marked the boundary between the ladies' and gentlemen's quarters; for the rest every one was free to pick and choose a nook to his mind on the benches or alongside them, behind a cabin or out on the open deck, there to stretch his mattress and await the cessation of the chatter, then to become aware of the monotonous thud of the engines and to be wafted to the realms of slumber. There could be no question of having a long lie! For every morning at five sharp the swarthy brown sailors appeared with brooms and pails, to hose and scrub the deck most thoroughly. It was good fun then to walk about barefoot on the cool wet planks, lightly clad in pyjamas, until towards 7-30 the ladies gradually began to appear, forcing us to beat a retreat. A light meal, consisting of tea, coffee, bread and butter, the so-called *Choti Haziri* could be partaken of, Indian fashion, any time after 6 o'clock. At 9 followed a substantial breakfast, tea, with fish, eggs, meat, &c. The rest of the forenoon was of course spent on deck—some of the passengers sit or recline in their chairs, here a group indulges in gay conversation, yonder there are a number of people deep in their books, others again energetically pace the deck, trying their best to combat the worst evil of a long sea-voyage, the want of exercise—some care is however necessary to avoid treading on the numerous children calling everywhere. Children under seven may accompany their families to India without running any risk, but after seven they usually have to be sent back to Europe, the Indian heat proving deleterious to their development, as it produces both loss of appetite and sleep. Dinner was at 2 P. M. for the second class passengers, tea at 4; at 5 it was an amusing sight to watch the children having supper under the supervision of nurses or mothers; supper was served for the grown-ups at 7, and a last cup of tea at 9 P. M. The table was abundant, though the quality of the food frequently left much to be desired. One great blessing was the generous supply of ice at all times—it is prepared in the Freezing-room, which is under the supervision of a special officer, and in which, in spite of the tropical heat, such intense cold prevails that a sailor who happened to get locked up in it is said to have been frozen to death. The hours after supper were variously spent ; sometimes there was a dance on deck, sometimes a concert to which the other class passengers were solemnly invited, we even soared upon one occasion to the giddy height of a fancy dress ball, families going out to reside in India being equipped with all such frippery. On the whole, we did not find our fellow-passengers very congenial, far less so than on our home voyage, when we took a ship coming from Australia, meeting on it people who had wound up their business in Australia, and having gained their experience were on their way home either to retire altogether or to spend a well-earned furlough. The passengers on the voyage out were, on the contrary, mostly young and rather boisterous—here a certain bumptiousness was noticeable which will come over the young Englishman when he finds himself on his way to India as a merchant or government official with a relatively high salary. These young people, with whom the ship was packed, struck me with their noisy doings much as birds of prey would have done, ready to pounce upon their victims. Their loud games, drinking bouts and dances, would allow of no comtemplative moods, no deeper conversation ; triviality reigned supreme. There was nothing for it but to put up with it ; fortunately it could not last for ever. The repeated stopping of the engines, which even happened on our hot sail through the Red Sea, and sometimes lasted a whole day, gave rise to serious uneasiness as to when and how our goal was to be reached. After a three days' voyage through the Red Sea, however, and after having left Mecca and Medina with the sea-port of Jedda on our left, Suakim with Massaua and many another inhospitable and perilous shore on our right (we saw absolutely nothing of all these places however) MOCHA of coffee fame rose up on our left and we might now hope to reach Aden before long and get out of the furnace of the Red Sea into the fresh and airy Indian Ocean. We got safe past the Gate of Tears, *Bab-el-Mandeb* on which many a proud ship has struck and sunk, a mast projecting here and there above water, serving as a *memento mori* to the travellers who sail past. Late in the evening we cast anchor in front of Aden for a few hours, and saw the buildings on the shore and the sun-baked arid mountains behind them lying in the magic light of the moon. Before retiring to rest on deck I had gone down into my cabin for a little and turned on the electric light when, looking out at the open port-hole, I saw a couple of black faces with gleaming eyes and flashing white teeth before me. They were Somali negroes who, defying quarantine under cover of night, had rowed out in their boat to the ship and were offering all sorts of curiosities for sale at the cabin windows, which were but a few feet above the level of the surface of the water. For a comparatively moderate sum I purchased a bottle of parti-coloured straw and a fine pair of antelope's antlers, which I managed to get rid of later on by making a present of them, after having dragged them about with me for some time in India. Next morning found us in the more breezy region of the Indian Ocean. For half a day we had still the gradually receding but beautifully shaped mountains of the south coast of Arabia on our left; then for seven whole days we entirely lost sight of land. It was re-assuring however to learn that the *Himalaya* had not transferred her mail to one of the other steamers running between Aden and Bombay—we drew the inference that in spite of the delay incurred, and in all probability still to be incurred, there was still hope of getting the mail to Bombay before it was overdue, in case of which eventuality the Company has to pay a heavy penalty. For the rest we steamed on more and more slowly, and repeatedly the steamer had to be laid to for a few hours on the glassy ocean, while numerous sharks gambolled about the vessel, greedily snapping up the kitchen offal. One afternoon, when we had again come to a stop, some sport-loving Englishmen passed the time fishing for sharks with a big hook, attached to an anchor chain, baited with a piece of meat, and they actually succeeded in getting one of these monsters on board. It lashed about it so terribly when being pulled in, that its tail had to be hacked off before the fish could be got on deck. There it lay, more than six feet long and as fat as a prize pig; it took some time before it began to calm down, surrounded at a respectful distance by a circle of inquisitive spectators. The monster had already been disembowelled, and its heart, no bigger than a watch and still beating, was being handed from hand to hand, but still the leviathan possessed strength enough to roll from one side to the other, to the horror of the lookers-on, who retreated precipitately. At last the shark lay dead and motionless. After a considerable piece of his skin had been cut off as a keepsake the rest was about to the thrown into the sea, when some of the ship's negroes stepped forward and asked for the fish. It was gladly given them and they dragged it off exclaiming in their nigger English "Shark eats nigger, why not nigger eat shark?"

With these and the like pastimes the days went by and at last on Sunday, November 6th, about noon, we saw the lofty ridges of the Ghatts chain towering in the east. A few hours later the azure blue of the ocean turned to a dirty yellow, the villas of Malabar Hill on the left, and the palm-wreathed towers and palaces of Bombay in front of us grew more distinct, and towards evening we rounded Colaba Point and cast anchor in the wide harbour of Bombay, separated from the open sea in the west by the mighty peninsula or island on which the Town of Bombay lies. We were soon surrounded by a swarm of steam-pinnaces, sailing boats, whose high bamboo yards were on a level with our decks, and all kinds of other vessels, and an indescribable confusion now set in on board our ship in the rapidly growing dusk. Shore officials and hotel agents, boatmen and porters, as well as friends who had come aboard to welcome those arriving; add thereto 340 ship's passengers with their respective luggage, and the

361 souls who went to make up the crew, from the Captain down to the lowest galley-boys, stokers and lascars, all surging and moving about in one fearful topsy-turvy! Our friends too had come on board, but they looked for us in vain, as we had no intention like so many on board of taking the train inland that very evening, and had decided on spending the night on deck as usual. Having got rid of so many noisy fellow-travellers it was really the most pleasant evening we had spent on the *Himalaya* in spite of the oppressive sultriness, which was doubly felt now that the ship had ceased to move. Next morning we gave our luggage to the hotel servant, got into a boat, bade a grateful farewell to the leviathan that had so long sheltered us, and with feelings that are beyond words set foot at Apollo Bandar on the sacred soil of India. A quarter of an hour later we were installed safe and sound in the spacious rooms we had ordered beforehand in the Esplanade Hotel.

CHAPTER III.

Bombay.

WATSON'S Esplanade Hotel, in which we took up our residence for a few weeks, is looked upon as the first hotel in Bombay, and is one of the largest, if not the largest hotel in India. It is however by no means so typically Indian as the twenty or thirty other hotels we stopped at in our travels through all parts of India, which is no doubt to be explained by the close relations existing between that city and Europe. A short description of the typical Indian hotel may here follow, and I may mention that on principle—hygiene being no secondary consideration—we always went to the best hotel in the places we visited. To be sure this often happened to be the only one, and many of the places, *Ujjayini* (Ujjain), *Gaya* and others, did not even boast of one. In these cases the Government generally establishes a *Dak Bungalow*, in which the traveller may lay claim to a room with a bed in it on payment of one rupee per person, on the express condition that the room must be vacated should a newcomer arrive the following evening and fail to find accommodation. As a rule however one finds oneself the sole guest. The furniture is exceedingly primitive, the beds middling, though generally free from vermin, and not nearly so bad as those met with in Greece. Mosquito-nets, however, are generally wanting, and the traveller would do well to carry his own with him. The bed-clothes, *i. e.*, pillows, a thick quilt, (Razai) to lie on, and a plaid to cover oneself with, form a part of every traveller's luggage, being indispensable both on the railway and in the hotels, as well as in the *Dak Bungalows.* The bed-room doors in the Dak Bungalows are provided with very deficient fastenings, and in Amritsar, for instance, there was nothing for it but to barricade the door with what luggage we had. The cooking in the Dak Bungalows is generally very poor. A cook, or the Manager himself, provides the meals. There is usually a Government tariff of prices, but the quality depends on the capacity, goodwill and ambition of the cook, who is almost always a Mahomedan. We occasionally managed to get a good meal out of him on the recommendation of some friendly native, but we also experienced the reverse, as our story will show. The Refreshment Rooms of the smaller railway stations are very much on a par with the Dak Bungalows, and in places where there is either no Dak Bungalow at all or none near, you can generally manage to get a night's quarters in the Waiting-room. Should the Waiting-room happen to be occupied the obliging Station Master is quite ready to put a railway carriage at the disposal of the traveller. No charge is made in either case, but the expedient is not to be recommended ; shunting goes on incessantly, and when a train starts late in the evening, early in the morning, or during the night, the natives arrive in crowds hours beforehand and squat round about the station-house in Indian fashion on the bare earth, chatting in groups; the air gets very bad and the noise is unbearable.

However you are seldom reduced to such an extremity, as in all tolerably frequented places there are fair hotels, almost exclusively kept by English people. The prices are very moderate. It is the custom as in Spain, Palestine and Egypt, to make a daily charge for board. With the exception of Bombay, Calcutta and Darjeeling, in the first hotels the board was never more than five rupees for the room and three ample meals, though never less either. This uniformity of price makes it possible to calculate the cost of a journey to India pretty accurately beforehand. A second-class return ticket available for six months, food included, costs £50, the first-class railway ticket throughout India about £25, four to five months' hotel expenses amount to about £50, and by calculating another £25 for wines, luggage, carriages, trips and attendance, it will be found that a journey to India may be made for about £150, if economy has to be strictly observed, but for anyone with bigger pretensions can be comfortably accomplished for about £200. A letter of credit is the most convenient way of carrying money, and on it, as in all the larger towns of Europe, cash payments are made in Bombay, Madras, Calcutta and Colombo. The coin of the country is the rupee, a silver piece about the size of our 2 Mark piece, which is in India divided into 16 annas, in Ceylon into 100 cents. The anna again is made up of 4 paisas (copper coins about the size of a sou) the paisa has 3 pies, and the tiny shells call Kapardika in Sanscrit, but now known as Kauri, still represent the smallest currency. I got 80 of them at the Benares market in exchange for one paisa, which would make 5120 for a rupee. Gold is never met with, but you find bank-notes for 10, 25, 50, 100, 500 rupees and even for larger amounts. In the Lahore Bank I was even allowed to handle a 10,000 rupee bank-note, differing very slightly from the 10 rupee notes, except in the figures stamped on it.

The Indian hotel generally lies, like all better-class houses, outside the native town with its narrow streets, on a broad and well-kept road, and stands, like all the neighbouring private dwellings and houses of business, in a spacious garden of its own. The hotel is usually one-storied; the big dining-hall occupies the centre of the house, cool, sometimes even dark; round about it are the bed-rooms with doors opening into the dining-room as well as direct communication with outside. Outside the bed-rooms a verandah runs round the house, and on it the personal attendants of the travellers sleep. In cold weather they wrap themselves up in their own bed-clothes head and all, so that they closely resemble long bulky sacks, and it is only the heavy snores that reveal them to be human beings. The bed-rooms are generally very spacious, the furniture scanty, utensils and towels like everything else in India old and tattered. Each bed-room is provided with a toilet-room with a washstand, bath and other conveniences, and the only persons having access to it from the outside, besides the inmate of the bed-room to which it is attached, are the water-carrier and the sweeper, who are always at hand to put things in order after use. The bath is mostly nothing but a piece of cement with a high rim running round it and an opening to the outside to let the water out, which generally has a grating to keep out snakes. Glass windows are limited in number and in some places are conspicuous by their absence. The manufacture of glass had not yet, we were told, been introduced into India. All bottles are imported from Europe, and it is no uncommon sight in the street to see a pedlar retailing a goodly assortment of old wine, beer and lemonade bottles. The doors, as aforesaid, are deficient in locks, but you find in their place large iron bolts both outside and inside. On leaving your room you can lock it, but so insecurely that anyone can manage to get in. Yet great security prevails in India, more especially as every house is more or less surrounded by servants day and night.

The culinary arrangements in the hotels are usually both ample and good, and the danger of injuring one's health by injudicious indulgence in the pleasures of the table is far greater than the risk of meeting with tigers and snakes, or getting a sunstroke, &c. This is more especially the case for those who, like the Englishmen, drink their whiskey and soda every day with a tendency to reduce the quantity of the latter element to a minimum. French claret and hock can be had everywhere for about a rupee and a half per half bottle, half a bottle of Bavarian beer costing half a rupee. It is best to avoid all alcohol in such a hot climate : as a rule we drank sparkling lemonade at meals and found it suited us exceedingly well. The repasts resemble those served on boardship Chota Haziri (tea and bread and butter) brought by the servant to your bed-room in the morning before you get up, a copious breakfast with all kinds of meat dishes served in the dining-room between 9 and 10 o'clock, tiffin, the English lunch, in the dining-room at 1 p. m., and consisting of various cold meat courses, and towards evening an ample dinner of soup, fish, meat, poultry, vegetables, sweets, &c. Fruit is never wanting on the table ; in winter mostly bananas and oranges, later in Ceylon about the beginning of March we had pine-apples and delicious mangoes, a kind of plum about the size of a goose's egg ; two diametrical cuts on either side of the stone divide it into three pieces and you scoop out the juicy aromatic pulp with a spoon.

The chief inconvenience in the Indian hotels is the attendance. There are, it is true, plenty of servants both in the dining-room and for the rooms, but they are little used to attending to travellers, as almost every one travels with his own servant. Such a servant gets 20 rupees a month, and on this he lives, and dresses, being no doubt able to save the half and send it home to his family. Besides his wages he gets a 3rd class railway ticket, which is surprisingly cheap, about one-seventh of the first class fare, and for a few rupees he is carried from one end of India to the other, though in by no means enviably packed carriages. Such a servant is very useful, nay even indispensable to the new-arrival. He is, in general, familiar with the whole of India, acts as a go-between with the natives, arranges with carriages and porters, and helps the traveller when shopping, though here he openly claims and receives a percentage from the salesman. In the train he provides refreshments, makes the beds at night and packs them up again in the morning. In the hotels it is he who makes the beds in the rooms, and who waits on his master at table, entering the kitchen without let or hindrance, and catering as best he can for his employers. At night, even in the depth of winter, when however the cold is not severe, he sleeps in the open air on the ground in front of his master's door and in the morning he is there ready to answer the first call. He accompanies his master on all his expeditions, is familiar with all manner of situations, and speaks broken English which is sometimes excessively funny. This is the ideal of an Indian travelling servant, but the actual article is often very far behind that ideal. We had omitted to have a reliable servant engaged for us either by friends or other persons of confidence, and, in consequence, were not exactly lucky in our choice. We had scarcely arrived at Watson's hotel when an individual in clean native dress made up to us, showed us to our rooms, and from that moment refused to quit us. It was Lalu, our first servant. At first we thought he was one of the hotel servants, and did not entirely grasp the situation until his efforts to make us comfortable had reached a point which, in my opinion, made it impossible for us to dismiss him without some weighty reason ; such a reason presented itself in the course of our journey, as we shall see a little further on. What particularly took my fancy in Lalu was the fact that he was a genuine Hindu and not a Mahomedan. I had overlooked the fact that only the very lowest caste of Hindus will condescend to serve Europeans, a caste even more strenuously avoided by the higher classes than Christians or Mahomedans. Our Lalu did not dare to cross the threshold of our Hindu friends, for a general house purification would have been the necessary consequence of the pollution his very presence would have brought upon the house. All carefully avoided any contact with the fellow, who was both clean and good-looking. One day I was sitting in my room in Bombay with my Pandit Veniram, having my Sanscrit conversation lesson, while Lalu was busy tidying the apartment. It struck me that the Pandit kept looking anxiously about him, and that he fidgeted. In reply to a question he said " If that person were to touch me I could not return to my house without having first taken a bath and changing or washing all my clothes." This fear entertained by the orthodox Hindus of being polluted by touching a Cûdra properly extends to all Europeans who are on principle all Cûdras. However the force of custom has so far conquered that almost all Hindus will shake hands with a European; it was very rare to find them refuse to do so. The less enlightened circles are more anxious about it, the women, in particular, who, when you meet them in the streets, are in the habit of drawing their garments more closely over face and bosom and making a wide detour to avoid the European.

But let us return to Watson's hotel, which chiefly differs from the hotels above described of inner India by making a more European impression. It is most imposing in appearance both in and from the outside, standing apart from the other houses in the finest quarter of Bombay, not far from the Government buildings and the sea, with its fourteen windows in front and its four stories. The ground-floor is occupied by shops, post and other offices; on the first floor are the large dining-rooms, in which the punkah is kept going above the heads of the dinners, summer and winter; the folding doors stand wide open, and lead on to a big terrace where coffee is partaken of after dinner, and the visitor looks down on the open square in front of the hotel, on which a motley Oriental crowd is surging. You can see Hindus of all castes and from all parts of India, position, trade, and district being recognisable to the practised eye by the clothing. There are Parsees, Mahomedans and Europeans, half-castes, Jews, Christian converts, all characteristically differing in costume. Nor are shows wanting, snake-charmers, men with monkeys, dogs, other animals performing their tricks to the sound of the drum and the rattle of the money-box in which the silver and copper coins that are thrown from above are collected.

In spite of these numerous distractions, despite the beautiful situation, the comfortable arrangements, and the excellent table, our stay in Watson's hotel cannot be said to have been a particularly pleasant one. There was a constant going and coming; every week, on the arrival of a fresh steamer from Europe, the hotel was crowded with restless guests who disappeared a few days later bound for the interior. Even at night perfect peace cannot be said to have reigned. There was a constant tramp of feet in the passages, a banging of doors, loud shouts of "Boy" (the English use the word in addressing the servants) till midnight and even after. If we closed our bed-room door and only opened the big French windows, the heat—25° by day and 20° by night—in consequence of the absence of a draught prevented us sleeping. If we opened both door and windows as far as possible, the conversation and snores of the servants in the passages, and the inconsiderate behaviour of the other visitors kept disturbing us. On this account, and because we desired to be nearer our friends, during our second stay in Bombay we preferred to live at a native club, which shall be described later on.

We had scarcely been two hours in the hotel when half a dozen natives came to call on us. To be sure our only Bombay acquaintance, Mansukhlâl Nazar, was away from home in Calcutta, where we met him later on, but he had charged his brothers, the staid and venerable Atmarâm, and the lively and amiable Utsavlâl, to look after us. They appeared, accompanied by an Indian prince, Baldevi, who like the others wore European dress, the only difference being that a mighty turban adorned his head, precious rings in his fingers and ears. Not being sufficiently familiar with the English language to be able to follow the conversation, he was in the habit of spending his time with the chewing of Tambulam, the various ingredients of which he always carried with him in a big silver box. He was attended by his young nephew and some other persons, so that our wish to get to know natives was not long in being accomplished.

Our first care was to order the letters of introduction according to the towns, and get out those destined for Bombay. The paying of various calls was then discussed, all sorts of excursions planned, and interesting persons mentioned whom our friends promised to bring to see us. In general the natives are not fond of receiving visitors in their own homes, partly because these homes are often but scantily furnished, partly too on account of religious scruples. They are however all the readier to come and see foreigners in the hotel, and not a day passed on which we had not a circle of natives about us, both in the morning and the afternoon.

Many wore European dress, but most of them, the Pandits in particular, appeared in native costume. They do not remove the turban or whatever headdress they happen to wear, lest the one long lock of hair allowed to grow on their otherwise closely cropped heads, as prescribed by their religion, should fall down. On the other hand, those wearing native dress invariably remove their shoes at the door and appear in the rooms in their stocking-soles, if not bare-footed. Being accustomed to squat cross-legged on the floor, they find chairs uncomfortable, and I often noticed how in the course of conversation they would draw up first one leg and then the other, until they had succeeded in getting into their customary posture (known as Padmâsanam) on the seats of the chairs. In conversation they are lively and pleasant, always full of curiosity, naive, and at times witty. If there are a number of persons together the conversation is apt to become noisy and confused.

A description of Bombay, next to Calcutta, India's biggest and finest city, may be considered superfluous. Its splendid situation on a promontory between the open sea in the west and the broad lake-like harbour in the east, the southern European quarter with its numerous fine buildings, the native quarter to the north with its narrow streets and incredible bustling life, have been often enough the subject of description.

Like most Indian towns, Bombay stretches away out to the north, the distances are often very great, but there is no lack of conveyances. There are plenty of horse-tramways, the horses wearing proper sun-bonnets to protect them from sunstroke; the cars, open on all sides and generally crowded, afford the best of oppórtunities for most interesting studies of native types and costumes. Then there are quantities of carriages, that have not infrequently some difficulty in making their way through the crowded streets, elegant private equipages drawn by horses which are mostly imported from Australia, besides the most heterogeneous collection of cabs, from those of the most elegant type down to cheap and humble Ekka, used by the natives only, provided with a single seat on the floor of the vehicle and mostly drawn by oxen, which are driven by a cord attached to their muzzles, and trot through the streets at a comparatively rapid pace. There is besides a local railway, which runs west from Bombay along the coast to the north past Malabar Hill out to the country, with about half a dozen stations. Malabar Hill is a ridge running out into the western sea to the north of Bombay, and on the harmonious wooded heights of which rise the Towers of Silence, the celebrated Parsee tombs, as well as numerous villas and temples. It was the goal of the first excursion we undertook with our friends one evening. The formidable sun-god had sunk into the western sea and "at one stride came the dark," when we reached Malabar Hill where a little popular festival was being held in the native quarter. Everywhere we saw people squatting in front of their houses, and, as is the custom in India, numerous little lamps filled with cocoanut oil were burning out in the streets in the open air, which was absolutely still. To our astonishment we saw numbers of almost entirely naked people moving about among the lamps and approaching us. It had been our intention to go and see a saint who had numerous admirers who looked up to him as a kind of spiritual adviser. He was just returning from an expedition and the crowd respectfully made room for the vehicle on which he sat with a companion, who kept chanting a few verses of the Veda in a low voice before him. The vehicle turned into a spacious court and one of our friends followed to procure us an audience. After some demur it was accorded us, on condition that we should remove our shoes. This we did, a proceeding which we repeated more than once on similar occasions later on. I soon got to find this custom to be such a blessing in the Indian heat, that I often took off my heavy boots uninvited and sat down in my stockings on the carpet among the natives, who were always exceedingly sensible to this observance of their custom. The saint sat cross-legged upon a raised divan, surrounded by a circle of worshippers, and my wife and I took our places on the carpet at a respectful distance from him. We entered into conversation, but the holy man spoke his Sanscrit so quickly that much escaped me, and one of those present had more than once to pick up the thread of the conversation in English. We spoke principally of Veda questions. Professor Peterson, to whom I lamented about this the following day, comforted me by telling me that these holy men often speak exceedingly poor Sanscrit and attempt to conceal their faults most skilfully by speaking very quickly. He by the way procured me a young Pandit, who came to the hotel to me every day and gave me conversation lessons.

Venirâm, as the young scholar of twenty-five was called, was the perfect type of an Indian pandit. He was absolutely ignorant concerning Europe and things European. He did not know a word of English, close as the study of that language would seem to lie for the Indian now-a-days, in fact, he abhorred it as something secular and impure, and this fear of polluting himself with anything foreign even extended to the use of Latin letters. When in speaking to him of my purposed journey through India, I unfolded the map he was not able to read a single name himself. He was all the more at home in his own world, though he kept back much that he evidently considered too sacred for me. Like all grown up Indians he was married, but had left wife and children in his native village and had come to Bombay to earn a scanty living in the English College Library, by comparing manuscripts and compiling catalogues. His father had, like so many Indians of ripe age, severed all earthly ties and had gone to Benares there to live as an ascetic. Venirâm gave me a letter of introduction to him, but by some accident this letter never reached the person to whom it was addressed, but fell into the hands of another ascetic, of whom I shall have to tell you later. In

Bombay, Venirâm lived a life strictly in accordance with his religion; he got up every morning at 4 o'clock, and, after having meditated for a short time on his patron divinity, took his morning bath, painted his red caste-mark upon his brow, said his morning prayer, the so-called Puja, all details of which he refused to communicate, read a chapter of the Upanishads and then, without having broken his fast, turned to the duties of the day. His two meals were taken one at 11 a. m., the other at 8 p.m. He prepared them himself, having no other member of his caste at hand, and it was he who did the house work as well as the washing and mending of his own clothes. His costume was of course strictly Indian; besides the imposing turban, and the shoes he always left at the door, it consisted of a number of cloths, mostly of thin white calico. The characteristic part of the Indian costume is the total absence of trousers, the place of which is supplied by a long strip of material ingeniously wound round the loins and legs. The upper part of the body was draped in the same fashion and the costume was completed by a handsome Cashmere woollen shawl. Many Hindus can dispense entirely with a tailor for their clothing; the majority, however, make use of a kind of great-coat with sleeves which they wear in cooler weather. With the exception of this article of clothing every bit of the costume is freshly washed every day, the Hindus on that account generally looking exceedingly clean and dainty; the bath twice a day effectually preventing any odour whatever, though it must be acknowledged that they are quite indifferent to a tear here and there in their wrappings. The women's dress in Southern India is still more simple, it is often limited to a single piece of material, either white or red in colour, black in the case of widows; this generally covers the whole body, but the head in particular; when at work it is caught up in such a way that the arms and the legs below the thigh are seen in all their nakedness, which gives a very graceful appearance to the Indian women, who are both beautiful and delicate in shape.

My pandit came every day, though in the beginning the hotel servants had once or twice refused him admittance. We read and spoke Sanscrit with great zeal, and I am greatly indebted to him for these preparatory exercises. At our last lesson I handed him twenty-five rupees, which made about one rupee for each lesson. I have been led to believe that he considered this modest remuneration princely by the attachment he continued to display during the remainder of our first, and during our second stay in Bombay.

Our mode of living in Bombay was as a matter of course regulated by the nature of the climate. We rose and made a hasty toilette at 6 in the morning, when the first sunbeams came peering through the luxuriant green leaves of the great trees, when the croaking of the crows as they flew from tree to tree mingled with the tender chatter of the little green parrots and the twittering of the numerous other birds found in India. A walk was then taken in the fresh morning air, generally along the sea-shore on the west where a splendid broad strip of land, affording delightful walks, extends between the town and the sea ; it has been wrested from the sea by the exertions of the English who have somewhat presumptuously given to it the name of Reclamation, as if the ocean had really owed them this strip of land. We could here watch the Parsees at their morning prayers ; they were easily recognised by their high black brimless hats, and while murmuring prayers would throw themselves on the ground, sprinkling their foreheads and members with the sacred dew. Or we sometimes went to Malabar Hill, where the Hindus knelt before their gods in the countless temples, paid the priests who spoke the prayers for them a few copper coins, and bathed in the adjoining tanks. Among other curious religious exercises I noticed an old woman, who kept sprinkling water from a vessel while murmuring prayers, and staring fixedly at the sun. My friends assured me that she had done this for twenty years without her eyes being any the worse, *Credat Judaeus Apella.*

At 9 o'clock we were glad to be back in the hotel for breakfast, the heat steadily increasing. The rest of the forenoon was devoted to work, unless visitors chanced to put in an appearance. How quickened in such circumstances does the study of Sanscrit become. What concrete forms do the Rig-Veda and the Upanishads, the Indian dramas and novels assume, where everything is so present to the senses. I hope the time is not too far away when every German student of Sanscrit will be able to pay at least one visit to India during his life time.

After tiffin we generally rested during the midday heat, and were disinclined to receive callers. About 4 o'clock our friends used to appear, we could take light felt hats in place of the heavy topees, and sally forth into the town or its environs. One of the most charming excursions is the one to Elephanta, an island in the eastern harbour, a good hour's distance from Bombay. Its rock-bored, half-subterranean temples are famous, and despite the havoc wrought by the Mahomedans there is still a goodly quantity of pillars and sculptures extant. One Sunday afternoon a party of twelve of us, all natives except my wife and self, got into a sailing boat; our cheery Utsavlâl had had all things pertaining to a Hindu meal taken on board in baskets, he himself appearing dragging a concertina. The wind wafted us across the smooth surface, to the strains of Hindu songs, past the town, houses, factories and wharves, to where the island towered out from the waves. A fine staircase led up from the shore to the temple caves, which are situated about half way up the height. I looked however, in vain for the serpents which, according to my friend Garbe's tales, ought to have been met with. We reached the temples without either difficulty or danger, and inspected the colossal reliefs carved out of the rocky walls, and with reproductions with which the reader is no doubt familiar, until the light, which penetrated from one side only began to fail us, and twilight enshrouded these stone witnesses of Indian religious art. Outside, in front of the temple we partook of the Hindu repast, and even the contrary wind that rendered our return a hardy one did not succeed in wearying the prevailing gay spirits of the party. At home a man of any gravity would be none too ready to indulge in such harmless pastimes, but here it afforded a welcome opportunity of observing the habits peculiar to a strange people in their own land. Thus day after day we became more familiar with the Hindu customs and way of thinking, and as our tale proceeds I shall introduce much of what we noted.

Something may here be said of the funeral rites, which are characteristically different for the members of each of the three religions to which the inhabitants of Bombay chiefly belong. The Mahomedans bury their dead as we do, the Hindus burning theirs, and the Parsees exposing theirs to be devoured by the vultures. Both the latter rites shall be more nearly described.

In Bombay, the Hindu Burning Ghaut lies to the west of the town, near the Marine Lines Station, not far from the sea. It is a big piece of ground with a high fence around it, and from outside a "pillar of cloud by day and a pillar of fire by night" may be seen rising from it. Strangers are admitted if accompanied, and from a space, reserved for the bearers and mourners, the burning process may be watched in its various phases. It takes four hours to burn a body completely but as a rule several bodies may by seen burning at once, so that it is quite possible to gain an idea of the beginning, middle and end of the ceremony. Decomposition setting in very rapidly owing the heat, a dead body is generally wrapped in white cloths from head to foot and carried to the burning-ghaut by the bearers a few hours after death has taken place. Stout logs, one to two yards in length are piled up to about a yard's height on the ground, between four iron stanchions, firmly planted in the earth ; the corpse is then placed upon this pile and another layer of wood piled above it. Meantime, a small fire is prepared beside the pile ; in Bombay this fire is brought from the hearth of the deceased ; in Benares where many corpses are burnt that come from a distance, even a considerable distance, the fire has to bought from a low caste, representatives of which are always present. Certain ceremonies now follow ; in particular, one of the deceased's relatives, very often a boy of tender age, has to pour water from a pitcher on the pile, afterwards breaking the pitcher. The small fire which has been kept in readiness is now added to the pile, soon the flames blaze up and the corpse's limbs are consumed one after the other. In three to four hours all that is left of the body is a few bones and ashes. In Benares, these remains and ashes are thrown into the Ganges as it flows past : I do not know what is done with them elsewhere. A priest, who murmurs a few texts, or perhaps gives a small address, is only present by exception and on payment of a special fee. There is nothing very solemn about the whole proceeding. On one occasion only did I hear a woman lamenting her deceased husband; the people mostly look on in apparent indifference, sometimes chatting to each other quite cheerily. The Indians take death less seriously than we do: death for them is only a single station on the wandering soul's great progress.

The Parsees, who constitute a large and highly esteemed portion of the population of Bombay, have very different funeral rites. The Parsees are the descendants of the ancient Persians, who, when Islam conquered Persia with fire and sword, took refuge in the tolerant land of India, carrying with them their holy books. On certain conditions they were received, and at present form an important contingent of Bombay's richest merchants. As the language of the Avesta proves, the Persians were undoubtedly of Indo-Germanic origin, and in contrast to this fact it is extremely perplexing to find many of the Parsees in Bombay pronouncedly Semitic in type, reminding us of our own Jews not only in face and figure, but also in character and manners. Among my collection of photographs there is one of a group of young Parsee ladies, who with their voluptuous figures and in some cases great loveliness strongly resemble what we are in the habit of designating *une beauté juive* (a Hebrew beauty). We find in the Parsees the same untiring search after, and pleasure in, gain; the same obliging amiability and occasionally somewhat tiresome forwardness as in our Jews. How is this to be accounted for? I can only explain it to myself by supposing that, after Cyrus' conquest of Babylon and Assyria, the Persians entered into extensive intermarriages with the native Semitic population and that the indomitable life-power of the Semitic race has asserted itself throughout the generations down to the Parsees of our own day. The Parsees resemble the Jews further in their being minded to go in for progress and for reforms, in contrast to the highly conservative Hindus. They have exceedingly well organised schools, for girls as well as for boys, in which all branches of learning are taught in the Gujerati tongue; nor are gymnastics neglected. The Hindus are slowly following their example, but repeated visits to such institutions have left upon me the impression that the Hindu schools are far behind those of the Parsees. The Parsees too have broken with their traditions, by entirely abolishing child-marriages, though many of them question the advisibility of having carried out this innovation too quickly and suddenly.

We were fortunate enough to make the acquaintance of a very kind, elderly, Parsee gentleman, Mr. Chichgar. He not only introduced us to his family, but did all that lay in his power tó be of service to us. True, he declared himself prohibited from letting us see the Parsee Temple, in the interior of which burns the eternal sacred fire; but, on the other hand, he offered to take us to Malabar Hill to the Towers of Silence, the celebrated Parsee tombs. Early one morning, accompanied by a Parsee priest, he fetched us from the hotel in his carriage. We soon got to Malabar Hill, and now a pretty path led us to the top of the hill where the spacious Parsee grave-yard lies, with a wonderful view of Bombay and the sea. With its flowers and shrubs, and well gravelled paths, it has all the *solemn* peacefulness of a Christian Cemetery, were it not for the absence of graves. Instead you see a number of round towers at a considerable distance from one another, no higher than a two-storied house, but as big as a circus in circumference. A single iron door, which is always kept shut, leads into the interior, which widens out into a kind of plate-like open surface, open to the sky, and surrounded by walls about six feet high. This surface is divided into three parts by two concentrical circles, in each of which there are numerous circular furrows for the accommodation of corpses, the innermost circles being for children's corpses, the two others for those of adults. A model in the waiting-room at the entrance gives one an idea of the whole arrangement. No one is admitted to the towers, not even a Parsee, with the exception of the well-paid corpse-bearers, who however are looked upon as unclean, and avoided. They carry up the corpse, which is swathed in cloths, upon their shoulders, followed by the train of mourners. At a becoming distance from the towers a general halt is made, the last ceremonies are performed and then the bearers carry the corpse alone into the tower by the iron door behind which it disappears for ever from the ken of man. The mighty vultures, a number of which are always to be seen perched upon the edge of the tower, at once swoop down upon the body, and in less than half an hour the bones are picked clean. The bones left are after some time pushed down into a hole in the middle, where they are subjected to a disinfectant process and then washed down by the rains into the sea. The whole business has nothing at all repulsive about it, when performed as it is in a solemn and reverent fashion, far less repulsive at all events than the Christian custom of burial.

Of course, when in Bombay, as everywhere else in India, we were diligent in our attendance at the Hindu temples. With their idols, to which under the auspices and prayers of the officiating priest the people offer all sorts of flowers, milk, grain, &c., these temples give as adequate an idea as possible of the ancient Indian rite of sacrifice at the time of the Veda, a period at which neither temple nor idols were known and the sacrifices were presented to the invisible gods by the agency of the Agni, *i.e.*, the sacrificial fire. Such Vedic sacrifices are but seldom performed now-a-days, and then only in the strictest privacy. It was my great wish to be present at such a sacrifice. The matter was not altogether an easy one, the Brahmans to whom my friends applied repeatedly refusing to keep their promise when already given, alleging religious scruples. At last four were found who declared their readiness to arrange a small sacrifice in the garden of one of our friends at dawn. My wife and I were to be allowed to look on from the balcony of the house and in return I, (*as Yajamâna*) had to defray the expenses of providing the sacrifice itself, as well as the sacrificial fee (*Dakshinâ*) to the priest. When we arrived the ceremony had already begun. In the garden before us a square hole had been dug in the earth and rudely lined with stones. In it a bright fire was blazing, and round it squatted three Brahmans who purported to represent the *Hotar*, *Adhvaryu*, and *Udgâtar*, while a fourth, seated somewhat apart, directed the proceedings as Brahman. Round the fire were placed a large pot of melted butter, which on being poured in spoonfuls into the fire made it blaze up; farther a bundle of Kuca-grass and all kinds of grain and fruits arranged in little piles upon leaves instead of plates. The whole proceedings were limited to all three Brahmans without any distinction whatever, throwing the above-mentioned substances into the fire, bowing repeatedly towards the fire in their seated attitudes, and accompanying their action with the chanting of Veda verses. I distinctly recognised the Purusha Song. In half an hour it was all over, the honour remaining for me to pay twenty-five rupees for a spectacle which may have had but a faint resemblance with the actual ancient Vedic sacrifice, but which nevertheless lent some food to the imagination, as what we had seen, however mangled, may be traced back to ancient tradition.

The national Hindu theatre would appear to have retained more of its originality, more especially when ancient plays are performed, or plays written in imitation of the ancient ones. Our friend Vicvanâth was the author of such a play, the subject being *Harischandra's* extreme love of truth, which rises superior to all temptations. This piece was being played in Bombay at the time, and the author invited us to go and see it. Two seats of honour immediately in front of the stage were reserved for us; beside us sat the poet, to explain the action to us as the play proceeded; behind us a large audience, consisting entirely of natives. I did not see a single European face. The theatre, stage, and curtain did not differ very materially from a simple European theatre, such for instance as may be found either in Italy or in Spain. On the stage, to the right and left of the curtain, squatted two musicians; one played the melodies on a concertina, the other accompanied him on a variety of drums, which he beat most deftly either with his fist or the edge of his bare hands, while daintily nodding his be-turbaned head in time to the music. I have rarely seen a man so absolutely absorbed in his business as this drummer. The curtain rose; a chorus of boys dressed as girls sang the *Nândi*. Then followed the customary dialogue between the Sûtradhâra and the prima-donna; then came the piece, the dialogue being written in Gujerati, the frequent lyric portions being sung. All the parts were played by men and boys. The actors, who are born to the profession belong to a special, inferior caste of Brahmans; their play was very sure, and testified to careful training; the boys' voices in the dialogue and singing were clear and fresh, though tending somewhat to shrillness. The music, which had been specially written for the piece was typically Indian, and was not without a charm peculiarly its own. Here and there the composer had been led into introducing a European motive, which never failed to strike the ear and produced a somewhat incongruous and by no means pleasing effect. The piece, which was overflowing with noble sentiments, played of course partly in heaven, where the Council of the Gods was assembled, Agni, Indra, Varuna, and many other Gods easily recognisable by their traditional costumes. The wise Nârada approached their presence, was most ceremoniously received, reported what was happening on earth and was entrusted with the messages of the Gods to mankind. Other scenes play on the earth, at the court of the kings where Vidûshaka, easily distinguishable by his conventional costume, cracks all sorts of jokes, which are invariably warmly applauded; in the Harem of the king's wives; in the huts of the poor; in the hermitages of the forest. The chief merit of such a performance is perhaps the doubtless faithful reproduction of many scenes of Indian family life, which the foreigner would otherwise never have an opportunity of becoming acquainted with. Vicvanâth made use of an interval to take us behind the scenes; we were introduced to the Manager, saw the boys taking off the rings they had worn in their noses when playing princesses or other Indian ladies, and which were simply kept on by a spring. Refreshments were offered us, and before we returned to our places we had to consent to being hung with wreaths of flowers, a general custom when visits are paid in Indian Society. This was not our last visit to the Indian theatre; in Baroda, Lucknow, Calcutta, and on our second visit to Bombay, we again attended representations, but the impression made by the first piece we saw was the deepest, and is indelibly engraved upon my memory.

The time was now at hand when we purposed leaving Bombay. Once more we were seated in a circle of visitors in our hotel apartment, when a newcomer entered. As usual in such cases, without further interrupting the conversation I bade him sit down, when he cried out in great glee: "Don't you know me? I am Dhruva from Baroda, to whom you were so kind in Berlin. I read in the papers that you were here, and am glad to have found you out." "You must," he continued, "give me a few days when you pass through Baroda where I am Judge. Arrange to be there over a Sunday, for I shall be free and be able to devote myself to you." We readily accepted his invitation and the details were at once arranged. A few days later Dhruva wrote to us from Baroda that though the Prince of Baroda himself was absent, the Prime Minister of the tiny principality would be delighted to receive us as State guests.

CHAPTER IV.

From Bombay to Peshawar.

THE EVENING of our departure had come. Our friends had assisted us in procuring the necessary portmanteaux, a tiffin-basket, and the bedding without which no one would think of travelling in India; they had helped us to pack, and a number of them had come to spend the last hours with us. We were bound for the station. One of them drove us there in his carriage, another saw to the luggage, while the rest repaired to the station, there to give us a last cordial shake of the hand. I had fixed to start from the terminus Colaba, one of the five railway stations at which the night train stops, and got there with bag and baggage an hour before the train left, hoping in this way to get a compartment to my wife and myself. These hopes proved vain. We were, to be sure, among the first travellers to arrive, and there stood the train, with all the carriage doors open, but after walking up the whole length of the train we discovered that there was not a single first-class compartment left in which one or more places were not labelled *reserved.* This time we had to make the best of it, and established ourselves with our eight articles of luggage, which in India are all accommodated in the roomy carriages, in a compartment into which an Englishman of youthful appearance soon got in to take the place reserved. Our friends clustered round the door of the carriage, offering this or that refreshment. A box of grapes is the usual offering, as they do not grow in India proper, but are imported from Afghanistan, packed in round wooden boxes containing three layers of berries, imbedded in wadding. The station-master's whistle sounded, a last shake of the hand all round, and then the curtain fell upon the brilliant picture. "I have got to be friends with all these natives in the few weeks of my stay in Bombay" I remarked to the Englishman. "Very possible; but we have to govern them, and that is a different matter," he replied sententiously and significantly. He then lay down full length upon his lower seat, my wife took the seat opposite to him, being unable on this occasion to undress, and there was nothing for me to do but climb up to the upper berth. Sleep was hard to woo under these circumstances, the heat being very great in spite of all windows and ventilators being kept open. But we were northward bound and December was at hand, so we might hope for cooler weather.

Leaving our travellers to doze across Surat and the Narmadâ, as they pass through many a magnificent district in the dark, to find them at Baroda early the following morning, let us say a few words of the Indian railways. India is intersected by a perfect network of railways, which are excellently organised, like all purely administrative matters the English have to do with. In India, as in Russia, the gauge is broader than on our railways and the carriages are in consequence both larger and more comfortable. There are three classes, as well as an intermediate class between the second and third; carriages and tickets are of corresponding colour, so that the traveller has no difficulty in recognising the white First Class carriages from a distance. The fares are so graded that each higher class costs about double the one below it. The third class is surprisingly cheap, but at the same time terribly crowded. It is entirely given over to the natives, and it is very amusing, to see men, women, and children, with huge bundles on their heads, the smallest children seated astride their mothers' hips, crowding round the carriage doors with great clamour; not till one carriage is simply packed is another opened. There are special compartments for women. The Intermediate Class is a degree better, and here European faces are occasionally met with. Sometimes these compartments are variously labelled *Natives*, or *Europeans Only*. The better class natives, unless they happen to be princes, who have carriages of their own, and a great many Europeans, travel Second Class. In the First Class carriages single travellers are met with but they are not infrequently empty. We nearly always had a compartment to ourselves, and were very comfortable both on our day and night trips. A First-Class carriage contains only two roomy compartments, separated by a door which is generally locked. Each compartment is provided with a good lavatory, which takes up the end of the carriage. Each side of the compartment is taken up by a cushioned seat covered with leather, upon which the beds are made up at night. Two similar seats are attached to the roof and can, in case of need, be let down. As the railways guarantee sleeping accommodation for the night there are never more than four persons in a compartment at night, never more than six during the day. In most cases, as already mentioned, the traveller has a compartment to himself. With the exception of the Guard who travels in the train, there is no other official to be seen. The tickets are sometimes, though very seldom, inspected when the train stops at a station, and this is done by half-castes (half European—half Native) who are capable of very little else. The arrogance of their bearing is rather ridiculous, as they are in most respects unreliable, and cannot be said to encourage any farther mixture of English and Indian blood. The arrangements for food on the railways are exceedingly well regulated; breakfast, tiffin and dinner are ordered by telegram by the Guard beforehand at the appointed stations, where the train usually stops fifteen to twenty minutes. Under these circumstances it is quite possible to travel day and night by rail for some time (the express from Bombay to Calcutta takes three nights and two days), there being wide projecting roofs and wooden blinds to keep out the sun's hot rays.

It was at 8 o'clock on Sunday morning that we got out at Baroda, the capital of a little principality, whose ruler, the Gaekwar of Baroda, happened to be in England at the time, which however in no way interfered with his hospitality as far as we were concerned. Dhruva was at the station and drove us straight in a magnificent court equipage to the palace, in which we were to take up our quarters, and which is about five minutes' drive from the Gaekwar's chief palace. Here we were received by Herr Maier, a young south German, who acted as Manager or Steward of the Gaekwar's various palaces. In appearance and language he reminded us of home, but everything he showed us and placed at our disposal made us believe ourselves transported into the midst of an Oriental fairy tale. A magnificent reception-room with carpets, divans, and arm-chairs, a spacious and lofty, but yet cosy dining-room, two large bed-rooms, with first class beds and furniture, everything new, scrupulously clean, and in the best of taste; a pillared and arched verandah extending round the house, all this went to make up the fairy kingdom of which we were to be lords absolute for the next few days. The cook with his scullions, a number of servants to render the various services we stood in need of, perhaps a dozen in all, dressed in the most immaculate native dress, went noiselessly about their duties, attentive to the smallest sign or wish we intimated. Day and night a fine draught prevailed in the cool halls of the house, which stood by itself. Doors and windows were left open at night, as we knew ourselves to be properly watched over and guarded, the distant howling of the jackals, who did not fail to give us a many voiced concert here as elsewhere in India, serving only to enhance the comfortable security of our enchanted palace. These animals, not unlike our own foxes in size and appearance, are exceedingly timid and hence nearly always invisible in Museums and Geological Gardens; they are however only all the more audible. Their howling sounds as if twelve puppies, a dozen kittens, and a corresponding number of babies had got up a concert of united barks, mews and yells.

We were entertained in as princely a manner as we were lodged; it was not the first time in my life that I had dined at a prince's table but I have never met with choicer cooking than what we were here regaled with. One word sufficed for the best of French champagne and the noblest of Rhine wines to be produced, a liberality we were somewhat chary of indulging in however, partly on account of the climate, partly too as such treats were familiar to us at home.

We made use of the early hours of Sunday to pay a visit with Herr Maier to the chief sights of the residence. Very curious were six cannons which, we were told, were of massive gold, and if so they must have represented an enormous value, while bearing eloquent testimony to the fabulous wealth of former Indian rulers. A stable of noble horses was of greater interest as were also a troop of over twenty elephants, the former being kept in the fields in open roofed sheds. The elephants are perfectly tame and good-tempered, though a few of the bulls that had become dangerous were isolated from the others and securely picked with heavy chains. We were warned not to go too near, so that it was from some little distance that I noticed their temples which were sore and from which a thickish liquid oozed, a process which is often referred to in Indian poetry.

The day was passed in the most agreeable fashion partly in sight-seeing, partly in paying necessary visits to ministers and other officials of high standing. In the evening a performance was given in the theatre in our honour, the places of honour being occupied by us, while, the general public being excluded, we were surrounded by a select circle of invited guests. Many introductions and salutations took place. By my request, as I desired to see an ancient drama, Priyadarçika had been chosen, and Dhruva had been thoughtful enough to have a kind of summary of the scenes printed for us as an English programme. We were thus enabled to follow the play most comfortably, scene for scene. The piece was of course played in the Gujarati translation, but stage, costumes, choruses, dialogues, &c., so closely followed the Sanscrit text that I may infer the present Hindu theatre to differ very little from what it was in the days of Kâlidâsa. Early next morning we rode on an elephant to Macka, a pleasure palace about an hour's ride distant. It was just being put in order for the return of the Gaekwar. Under the guidance of Mr. Maier, who had to superintend the work, we went through the various reception halls and learned with some surprise that when the Gaekwar gives court entertainments here his consort is not present. Indian women are averse to quitting the narrow circle of their own homes, and seem to be quite happy under the circumstances. The apartments of the princess were, I must add, most sumptuously arranged. I was particularly struck by a variety of magnificent musical boxes, though there was but one grand piano and that a poor one. We finished with a tour through the gardens and park, amid which the palace lies—they have only been recently laid out, but under the Indian sky will not be long in developing into a perfect Paradise. Our elephant now carried us homewards, the morning sun beginning to make itself rather uncomfortably noticeable, and on the way friend Dhruva gave me some interesting information respecting the trees we saw. For the first time I was enabled to make the distinctions between the *Nyagrodha* (ficus Indica) and the *Acvattha* (ficus religiosa). They differ very considerably both in growth and foliage.

In the afternoon the minister had arranged for a reception for us to meet the chief officials. Circumstances happened to relegate this function to our palace, and so it came to look as if the whole Cabinet and half the University had appeared to pay their court to us. They were all intelligent, grave and courteous men, differing greatly from European men of note in their picturesque and costly garb, but in no way inferior to the latter, it seemed to me, in behaviour, which was both refined and discreet. We conversed most pleasantly on Indian and European topics for some hours, and took a highly contented leave of each other.

A visit to the Sanskrit College was arranged for

the next day. It unites in itself both Grammar-school and University and afforded a good picture of the course of learning followed by an Indian scholar. The enviable fluency in Sanskrit the Pandits possess, and which is unattainable for a European, is due to their beginning to learn Sanskrit at about the age of nine, and their going in for little else during the whole of a long and diligent life. They begin by learning words and grammar by heart—the Raghuvanca is then studied as the first bigger poetical work, the Kumârasambhava, the Maghaduta, as well as the dramas of Kâlidâsa and others follow. For a higher grade come the novels, Dacakumâracaritam and Kâdambari, as well as the more difficult epics. In the University courses the teaching falls into two branches: some spend their lives in the study of grammar, literature and poetry, while others study astronomy, medicine, law or philosophy, all according to the old Sanskrit books, hence the teachers of astronomy regard the earth as the centre of the created system with everything else revolving round it. Very few venture to adopt the Copernicus system, still fewer openly confess to having adopted it.

When we entered the stately College premises, the various classes had already assembled with their teachers in a large hall open on one side. As usual various poems of welcome were recited in Sanskrit and then presented to me. I was also presented with a long prospectus written in Sanskrit, in which the curriculum of the various classes was specified. I was asked to put questions, and for fear of offending any one of the departments had, will I, nill I, to propound one question in every subject, grammar, literature, astronomy, philosophy, law and medicine. These questions were answered by the pupils, or in default of them by their teachers. It was particularly striking that only the best students were ready to answer, even when my question was addressed not to them, but to others. On the whole, the matter proved to be somewhat of a show-off, and subsequently when I paid a visit to an Indian school I used to ask the teachers not to mind my presence but to go on quietly with their lessons. In Baroda, we had our first sight of what we were to become so familiar with later on, of teachers and pupils squatting on the ground. When writing the copy-book is held loosely in the left hand, the right wielding the pen. The Hindus are so accustomed to this mode of writing that they usually despise a rest for the copy-book should it be offered them.

A visit to a neighbouring palace with all sorts of weapons and crown jewels was less interesting than our visit to the College. It left me the conviction however that, despite the many treasures that have already found their way to England, there are still plenty left for the English Governors and residents to have presented to them, or should they have their scruples, to be presented to their ladies. I am far from lending credence to all that was related to me in this respect, but must remark that the accounts given me of a journey made by an English Prince, and the gentlemen of his retinue, at times recalled the proceedings of Verres in Sicily, as recorded in Cicero.

It was with particular interest that we accepted an invitation of Dhruva's in Baroda, more especially as Indian scholars are not always inclined to open their houses to visitors. Here as frequently on subsequent occasions I was reminded of the worthy Javerilâl's saying: "Simplicity is the type of our life." We encountered a modest simplicity in the furniture and arrangements of the house, which may correspond to what was the custom with us in the Middle Ages. Mrs. Dhruva and her children were present, while on the other side of the passage we could catch a glimpse of a number of other female figures seated in Indian fashion on the ground. It is typical of the Indians that they make nothing of sitting down on the ground, no matter whether in the house or outside, the absence of damp making it more possible to do so than it is in our country. Another visitor was present at Dhruva's, an Indian Music Master, a man of great gravity, evidently entirely devoted to his art. He presented us with a work he had written in Hindustani on the theory of Indian music, with passages quoted from Sanskrit poems. Unfortunately, he spoke neither English nor Sanskrit, so that our conversation with him was exceedingly limited. The conviction I had already gained, of there being far more in Indian music than our unschooled ears could perceive, was confirmed by the impression his sober, scholarly, grave personality made upon me. Indian music is exceedingly complicated in theory, and the enthusiasm with which I often heard pieces of music performed would seem to testify to its being as well calculated as our own music to elevate and delight the human soul.

Our stay in Baroda was so rich in pleasant memories that we decided not to leave before having had a photo taken as a lasting memento of the days spent together. The place boasted of a tolerable photographer and he promised to appear with his camera in front of our palace at 4 o' clock on the afternoon of the day before our departure. The palace was of course to figure in the background. Everybody duly appeared at the hour appointed, one of the chief members of the party being the gigantic elephant that had carried us to Macka. He appeared decked out with a splendid rug, his trunk, cheeks and even ears being elaborately painted, and accompanied by his retinue of five attendants. Another principal character, whom Herr Maier in particular was most anxious to have included in the picture, was the *Citra*, (signifying in Sanskrit the many-coloured), the Prince's tame cheetah, which had been trained to hunt the antelope. His art consists in overtaking the antelope when once sighted, in rapid bounds, and killing it by a bite in the throat; the hunter then takes possession of his game, which is thus left uninjured in hide or flesh. Herr Maier had done all he could to get the minister to arrange a cheetah-hunt for us. It did not come off, however, as in fact I had no great mind to witness so cruel a sight. The *Citra* however appeared to be photographed with us. He was driven up on an elegant little carriage, chained and with blinders on his eyes. He had a retinue of no less than three body-servants and we were warned not to go too near him. In addition to the elephant and leopard, there were present my wife and self, Dhruva with his wife and three children, Herr Maier with his inseparable companion his riding-whip, as well as a few other secondary personages. We were all ready, only one person was wanting, and one that could not be dispensed with—the photographer. He was sent for, but was nowhere to be found. We waited in vain till darkness set in, the photographer had simply forgotten us. Under these circumstances, especially as everyone was looking forward to being photographed, there was nothing for it but to put off our start till noon and arrange a fresh meeting for the next morning, when the picture did at last get taken. As I hold it in my hand it recalls the whole scene down to the smallest detail. Our palace, with its stately entrance and lofty pillared hall forms the background; in front of it stands the elephant, as quiet and sagacious as if he understood what was going on; four of his attendants stand at his head holding long lances. The elephant driver (*Mahout*) sits in front on his neck, holding as a symbol of office the little iron goad, with which the colossal animal is guided, and made either to move on, to stop or to kneel down. This takes place when people have to get up or get down. An energetic prick with the goad on the beast's head makes him kneel down slowly with a gentle grunt of dissatisfaction; the servants bring up a little ladder, which the elephant always carries hanging on one side for this purpose, you get up and find a broad surface on the top with room for four or six people. It is surrounded by an iron railing. In our picture the ladies are seated on it, *i.e.*, Mrs. Dhruva in correct squatting posture, and my wife, who is very evidently ill at ease in her unwonted position. Each of them has a Dhruva child on her lap, the eldest son sitting between the two and eagerly watching the scene. I am standing in front of the elephant, much bothered by the sun in my eyes, the photographer having insisted at the last moment on my taking off my hat. On the right is Dhruva in national costume, to the left a school-master, and Her Maier in riding-breeches, whip in hand, his eye glued to the leopard, which securely held by three keepers completes the picture on the left. The beast unfortunately managed to move its head, and has come out with three heads, which might make it pass for Cerberus. The influence of the tropical sun is seen in the hard lights and the sharp contrasts of the shadows.

That was the closing act of our stay in Baroda. After a solemn good-bye meal we took a grateful farewell of our excellent quarters and drove off to the station with a numerous convoy.

Our next stop, Ahmedabad, lies but a few hours by rail from Baroda. It was our first experience of travelling by day through the Indian scenery, and on this occasion the road lay through a particularly fertile region, called the Cârutara by the Indians on account of its fertility. It was the 20th of November and with delight we gazed upon the verdant and blossoming landscape as it glided past us with its giant trees and rich tropical vegetation. Here and there a crowd of monkeys could be seen sitting in the trees and cutting capers in the grass, perfectly indifferent to the train as it rattled past them. Tropical countries are by no means always the most fertile; a glance at the map on the contrary teaches us that there is a broad strip of land, extending from the west coast of Africa, throughout the Sahara, Egypt, Arabia and Central Asia as far as China in which, owing to a kind of counter change between the increased heat due to the cloudless sky and the cloud formation prevented by the heat, it seldom or never rains. It is consequently condemned by Nature to remain a desert despite the most magnificent sunshine. Egypt would share the same fate, were it not for the Nile's overflowing its banks, and the whole of the splendid country of India would be a desert were it not for the monsoons, which blow in winter from the North-east, bringing rain to all but a few spots on the East coast, but blowing from the South-west during the summer months from June to September, and lavishing upon India so rich a supply of rain that the country is amply provided for the whole year. Next to no rain falls in India during the whole winter, and, with the exception of one rainy day in Benares and two in Calcutta, we rarely saw a cloudy sky during our four months' stay in India, and scarcely ever saw a drop of rain. It was the rule for the sun to run his majestic course across a perfectly cloudless sky from 6 in the morning till 6 at night. In our country under similar circumstances everything would begin to wither after the lapse of a few weeks; in India trees and plants retain their verdant green all through the winter, owing to the vast quantity of moisture which collects during the rainy season, and with which the soil is saturated. A further consequence of the climate is that agriculture is less confined to certain seasons in India than it is with us. To ripen from the seed to maturity, corn, wheat, and similar plants require a few successive months of damp, warmth of soil and sunshine. What months happen to stand in the Calendar are a matter of indifference to the plant, and where, as in India, those conditions are fulfilled all the year round with the exception of the rainy reason, the grain once sown is ready at all times to grow and ripen. So we could often see the grain being reaped in one field, while in the neighbouring one the ear was just forming, and in a third the first fresh green was just appearing above the ground. India has in general, as I was told, two crops a year, one in winter, the other for those plants which stand less in need of humidity in summer, before the rainy season begins. When the rainy season, which begins at midsummer, is over, the trees are clothed in the freshest of green, which they retain throughout the winter. In India, you never meet with a landscape in which the trees, as in our country in winter, stretch their bare leafless boughs and branches forlornly skywards; in spring, I was told, the old leaves begin to fall, but only to bourgeon afresh immediately.

So, while at home snow and ice reigned supreme we enjoyed the finest summer weather, and were by no means inclined to agree with a fellow traveller of a pessimistic character who kept complaining of everything Indian, and who affirmed that he was heartily sick of the eternal fine weather.

We had got to the end of the journey from Baroda to Ahmedabad, which called forth this digression, and steamed into the station of what at the time of the Moguls was the biggest and finest city in Western India. Now-a-days after a long period of decay the population has again risen to 148,000 inhabitants, but there is no hotel, and the Dak Bungalow being at some considerable distance we preferred to take up our quarters in a room in the station buildings. We had only just got settled as well as we could in the scantily furnished chamber, when four young men appeared, to whom we had letters of introduction from our Bombay friends. They were soon followed by the father of one of them, the rich and worthy old Ranchodlâl, who being a magistrate was able to give us much valuable information. He told us, for instance, that Ahmedabad had recently begun to have water put into the houses, but that the operations were much impeded by the Hindus refusing to use the artificial pipes. They consider no water pure (in the religious sense) that is not obtained from Nature first-hand, and they often drink the stagnant water of ponds which are simultaneously used for bathing as well as for washing linen and kitchen utensils. It is entirely due to these abuses that cholera has not yet been stamped out in India, and that in the hot season it makes an annual round of the Indian cities, leaving desolation behind. However it generally attacks the poorer classes only, and, as I was frequently assured, does not attack a gentleman, *i.e.*, a person leading a sensible life. "In our town," Ranchodlâl explained, "we have made the remarkable experience that those quarters already provided with water pipes suffered exceedingly little from cholera, and so we may hope to get the better of the scourge in the course of time." Chatting on these and other topics, we took a drive round the town, paid a visit to Lake Kankariya, situated to the south-east of the town, prettily ensconced in a setting of wooded hills, and on our drive back entered some of the numerous mosques still standing, the walls of which are frequently composed of wonderfully carved and fretted stones. We finished up our day with a walk to the lofty long bridge that spans the Sabarmati. Here honest young Harilâl unburdened his heart to me. The English have cruelly decreed that the higher offices in the Indian Government Service are only open to those who have passed their examinations in England. "With diligence and my abilities I have no doubt," said Harilâl, "of being able to pass these examinations; nor, thank God, do I want the means, but the voyage to England would entail my being expelled from my caste and I cannot inflict this sorrow upon my parents and relations. I therefore see myself condemned to spend my life in a subordinate situation." I did what I could to pursuade him to overcome this difficulty, pointing to Dhruva in Baroda as an example. Dhruva had been in Europe and, after returning very quickly and unostentatiously, had succeeded in regaining admission to his caste on payment of a few hundred rupees, and after doing a slight penance. I trust that Harilâl and many other young Indians in a similar predicament will succeed, after having outgrown their own religious scruples, in overcoming those of their families, so that all the better posts in the country may not have to be left in the hands of Englishmen.

On returning to the station, in front of which I stood for a time enjoying the fresh evening air, I was vastly amused to witness a battle royal of words between two Hindu women. Each sat quietly in front of her hut, and while the one kept unfolding the cause of dispute in the loudest of voices and with much passionate eloquence, the other listened attentively in dead silence till her antagonist stopped when she in turn began to enumerate her arguments with the same long-winded loquacity. The ball of discourse was thus kept flying backwards and forwards until exhausted lungs brought about a restoration of peace.

The following day, the only one we intended to devote to Ahmedabad, was rich in impressions. First, our friends took us back to the Sabarmati to see the Hindus bathing, a spectacle we had various other opportunities of witnessing, best perhaps in Benares, of which more hereafter. Then we were taken to see the great Jaina Temple, one of the finest and most gorgeous in all India. Jainism, being like Buddhism, as is well known, an atheistical religion, the place of the pictures of the gods is taken by the seated statues of Jaina and his twenty-four predecessors, for the people cannot be got to dispense with idols. Jainism differs from Buddhism, which has been extinct in India for centuries, and which we met with only on the North and South frontiers, in the Himalayas and in Ceylon, in its not having become international. On the contrary, it is rather Hindu national and has therefore asserted itself in Bombay, Ahmedabad, as well as in other places. Brahmanism here again shows its astonishing force, and has almost entirely assimilated itself with Jaiïsm. The Jainas therefore are just as chary of associating with foreigners, as the Brahmans in particular of eating with them, and, contrary to their original principles, not infrequently object to strangers entering their temples and viewing their feasts, whereas you are quite at liberty to enter and examine any Buddhistic temple.

The Jainas are further often the possessors of great wealth, and in the course of the morning we paid a visit to a Jaina workshop in which splendid wood-carvings and wonderful carpets were being manufactured. In this carpet-weaving the chain is stretched from top to bottom. Behind it sit a row of boys. Opposite them on the other side of the chain stands a man, pattern in hand, and at his word of command the boys alternately weave short, bright-coloured, woollen threads through the chain, the ends of the threads standing out and forming a shaggy woollen mass. On its being smoothly cut afterwards, the right side of the carpet reveals the loveliest pattern. Carpets, as well as carvings, are made to order for America and other parts of the world. The prices were so high that we refrained from making any purchases. The fairly youthful owner, whom a few questions proved to be the young man Garbe described, appeared in no way to expect us to buy anything. As is customary, at the close of the visit he presented us with the Visitors' Book, in which we gladly entered the pleasure it had really given us to see the work being done.

From here we went to the Pinjra-Pol (Cage Bridge), an animals' hospital, such as exists in Bombay, Ahmedabad, and many other Indian cities. These institutes, the intention rather than the results of which must command our respect, are for the purpose of nursing aged and diseased animals till death puts an end to their misery, as well as buying healthy animals, cows in particular, and thus rescuing them from the hands of Mahomedan butchers. Horses and cows, goats and dogs, are the animals usually met with in them. In the hospital in Bombay we noticed a cart with a cage in it containing several monkeys.

They turned out to be bad-tempered beasts sent to the hospital by the families they had belonged to, and were to be taken to the forest and there set at liberty. The severely orthodox Hindu will take the life of no animal, nor insect, not even of a serpent. Should he happen to meet one in a place where it might prove dangerous, he catches it and transports it to some place or other where he thinks it can do no harm, and there he sets it free. There are numbers of old houses in India the walls of which are infested with snakes. The common people spare their lives, believing the spirits of their ancestors to be embodied in them. I was often assured that these snakes never touched an inmate of the house. It is a fact that a snake will go out of a man's way and only bites if provoked, that is to say if they are stepped on accidentally or in the dark. Snakes are rarely met with in the winter, which they generally spend in their holes in the ground; we only once met a snake in the open air during our four months' stay in India, though we saw plenty in the hands of the charmers and in the Zoological Gardens. During the hot season and more particularly during the rainy season, they are said to be by no means rare, and sometimes appear in perfectly unexpected places. Frau Doctor Hörnle, for instance, once met a snake on the balcony of her first-floor flat in Calcutta; how it ever got there remained a mystery, but it may have been brought in, in a basket of vegetables. Frau Doctor Hörnle told me of a fine surprise one of her friends got. He had collected a batch of snakes' eggs in his trunk, and on opening it one day he discovered a lively brood of little snakes, which the tropical heat had hatched.

To return to the Animals' Hospital at Ahmedabad, we found nothing but the domestic animals already mentioned. It would have been a charity in many a case, where the poor beast was crawling about in a diseased or maimed condition, to put its sufferings to an end, so that the end attained stands in somewhat strange contradiction to the great and noble intention. These institutes are kept up by liberal contributions, the cotton merchants in Bombay, for instance, having pledged themselves to give a certain percentage of their profits to the Pinjra-Pol. It can only be looked upon as a bad joke when we read of the Animals' Hospitals having a special ward for insects, and of negroes being kept, whose heads furnish feeding-grounds. The Hindus assured me that such had never been the case, and yet a Missionary in Bombay had once the effrontery to insist to me upon the truth of the statement. Of this I shall have to speak later on, but I may venture here to remark that it is prudent not to believe all that the Missionaries tell and write about India. It is a pet trick with them to put rare cases so prominently in the foreground that they appear to be the rule, and not the exception, giving in consequence a thoroughly distorted picture of the life of the Indian people.

We finished up our morning with a visit to the *Sâdhus*, a kind of Indian monks, who live together in a well-endowed monastery. A meeting of them was at once convoked in a spacious hall. Between fifty and sixty of them were present, but scarcely more than one or two of them had even a smattering of Sanskrit. The Indian Pandits speak of these well-fed idlers with contempt and are probably not far wrong in doing so.

In the afternoon we had two big meetings one after the other. One was a meeting of Pandits, at which Sanskrit was spoken, the other was held in a Club and at it many subjects were touched upon in English, and, in particular, I was asked to give information respecting education in Europe. Then songs from the *Gîtagovinda* and other poems were sung to the accompaniment of national instruments. My friends begged to be excused spending the evening with us, as they required to be present at a dinner of their own caste. I asked to be allowed to have a sight of it, and they consented, but only fetched me, intentionally it appeared, when the chief proceedings were already over. In a long narrow street in which only members of this caste reside several hundreds of persons had been regaled, squatting in long rows in the street. I saw a few late-comers and the remains of a finished repast, particularly those numerous little clay vessels in which the food is placed separately before each guest, and which have to be thrown away at once. New ones are provided for every meal, a whole thousand, we were told, costing only one rupee. I had the pleasure of being introduced to the host and some of his friends, and was offered a taste of all the dishe all of which I had of course to pronounce excellent.

Next morning we left Ahmedabad and were glad to leave our cramped and noisy railway apartment behind us. Our friends turned up at the station; one of them, the younger Dhruva, (a brother of our Baroda friend) who was a teacher of Sanskrit in Ahmedabad with the help of a map very aptly explained to me in the Meghaduta, (which I always carried with me when travelling, for the purpose of learning by heart), the various localities the cloud rested upon, on its journey through India, some of which we hoped to visit. The train came puffing in, a hasty farewell to our friends, and off we went northwards through new districts, which gradually assumed a more sterile character, announcing the vicinity of the Desert of *Maru*, which extended to our left in a breadth of 300 kilometers, dividing the Valley of the Indus from the plain of the Ganges. In the afternoon a few scattered mountain ridges became visible, among them *Mount Abu*, celebrated as a summer resort, as well as for its Jaina Temple, of which we only caught a passing glimpse. Night fell, and we were to reach Jaipur, our next destination, at 5 o'clock the following morning. I carefully asked the Guard to wake us in plenty of time for Jaipur. He promised, we undressed as usual and fell peacefully asleep. In the night I awoke. The light in our compartment had gone out, deep darkness reigned. I struck a match and looked at my watch.

A quarter to five; in a quarter of an hour we were due in Jaipur, where the train only stopped seven minutes. The Guard had forgotten his promise. In flying haste, and in the dark, for candles we had none, though we never travelled without them subsequently, we had now to manage to find and to put on stockings, boots and our other articles of dress, a match being requisitioned when things threatened to become desperate. My vest with our supply of money persisted for some time in being lost. At last we were ready, and it was high time too, for the train was already slowing down, and, with the help of the servant, we got out in time, bag and baggage, and then repaired to the very middling Hotel Kaiser-i-Hind. Meantime, "the dawn's left hand was in the sky," and from the hotel windows we had a perfectly magnificent sunrise, all the more cheering after the pitch darkness of the night and the fears we had been a prey to.

The chief sights of Jaipur are the old Royal Castle with its stables, and the summer residence of Amber, about two hours distant. Immediately on arrival the new-comer has a slip of printed paper presented to him, on which he indicates the day and hour he desires to see these things. Everything else is then arranged for him without any trouble on his part, and an elephant for the trip to Amber is even provided from the prince's stables. After having settled this matter we went for a morning walk to the town, which lies at some little distance unfortunately, the roads too being exceedingly dusty. The town makes a cheerful impression with its broad streets and houses painted pink; the inhabitants, the Rajputs, with their tall powerful figures, are the most imposing types to be met with in India. In the centre of the town lies a large market-place, on which doves are kept, as in Venice and Florence. We bought a little basket of grain and could soon enjoy the pleasure of seeing the dainty creatures fluttering about our heads and shoulders, confidingly feeding from our hands until an impudent billy-goat appeared and created confusion. My regard for the feelings of the native bystanders kept me from dealing with him as he deserved.

We now wended our way to the prince's gardens, in which tigers, lions, and other wild animals are kept in cages, a general custom, the monkeys being chained to tall posts and thus at liberty either to climb up to their little cages or down to the ground, where they would investigate the soil and its composition as far as their chains would let them, with a whimsical gravity all their own. Not far off lies the Jaipur Museum, an elegant building with rich collections, situated in fine grounds. I was particularly interested in a collection of clay figures representing Indian ascetics in their multifarious tortured attitudes. Indian asceticism is originally traceable to a true and lofty recognition of the evils of existence, which gives rise to the desire to subjugate the flesh by self-sacrifice and tortures of all kinds. This genuine asceticism is however but rarely met with. In the Himalayas above Haridvâr where the Ganges flows out of the mountains, many ascetics are said to be found. My friend Candrikaprâsâd had had the idea of joining us in the course of our journey in order to introduce us there; unfortunately he was prevented from coming, and so the idea had to be given up, as it would have been exceedingly difficult for a European to see much if alone. The genuine ascetics retire into solitary seclusion and take no interest whatever in Europeans. Very different in character are the ascetics who repair to the towns, and there make a show of their penitential exercises. I met quite a number of them in Calcutta on the banks of the Hooghli. Each of them sits beside his own fire, almost entirely naked, with a water pitcher, a few rags and some other miserable possessions beside him. He is surrounded by a number of curious spectators, who look on admiringly at the performance of his speciality and bestow an alms upon him. Their art is generally confined to trying to sit as long as possible in an exceedingly uncomfortable position. I saw one standing on one leg, the other being tied up to a pole; another was lying on a bed of pointed wooden nails. Many other extraordinary positions struck me in the Jaipur models. Almost all of them smear their naked bodies with ashes, let their long hair hang untidily about their faces and their nails grow the length of eagle's talons. Their expression of face is brutal and bestial, proving amply how little their asceticism has to do with spiritual motives. In fact, they are neither more nor less than beggars, who assume the guise of ascetics, and with their tricks stand much on a par with the fire-eaters and sword-swallowers at our own market fairs. Like them too they very soon ruin their health by the practice of their miserable profession.

The Jaipur Museum, which led me into this digression, affords a splendid view from its terraced roof over the town and surrounding plain, which is bounded on three sides by fine mountains. On one of these mountain sides there is a "Welcome" dug out in gigantic letters in honour of the Prince of Wales. It is perhaps the hugest inscription in the world, and is visible from the other side of the plain.

North of the city, in the mountains, lies the summer-residence of Amber, to which we made an excursion the following day. We first drove to the foot of the mountains, where the elephant awaited us to take us to Amber by an undulating path, bordered on either hand by niches containing all sorts of idols. The road strongly resembled that leading from Athens to Eleusis, and just as on the Eleusis road at a turn in the road, the Bay of Salamis opens before the traveller, here Amber lies on the shores of a charming lake, nestling at the foot of a picturesque height. The houses are for the most part deserted and all sorts of ascetics haunt them. The stately palace crowns the height, making the usual Mohammedan Palace impression with its various halls, harems and baths.

On the way back to Jaipur we passed a pond in which crocodiles were kept, and we had a sight of them being fed. Our servant brought a heterogeneous collection of meat offal from a neighbouring butcher for half a rupee, chiefly lights, liver and intestines. This was given to the keeper, who tied it all to a rope and let it down into the water, calling loudly to the crocodiles the while. For some time not a ripple disturbed the smooth wide surface of the marshy water. At last he drew our attention to something moving in the water at a distance, it was a gigantic crocodile slowly swimming beneath the surface of the water. Soon others came and at last in the depths beneath us we saw four of them phlegmatically opening their jaws and snapping at the meat. They gradually succeeded in tearing off one piece after another, till at length one of the monsters seized the whole of what was left and swallowed it.

A visit to the palace with its big open audience halls, the beautiful garden, and neighbouring stables, containing horses and elephants, completed our picture of this Indian residence.

We hastened home, various Pandits having announced their intention of waiting upon us. They appeared and with them some others, in particular one blind old Pandit with barely enough to cover him. Nature had however endowed him with a merry heart, as she so often does with the blind. Not knowing that he had been blind from his birth I sympathetically inquired to what accident his infirmity was due. His answer was genuinely Indian—"Some sin committed in a former state or existence is the cause," he serenely answered. The belief in the transmigration of the soul is still, as in days of yore, the foundation of the whole

Indian religion. It comforts the Indian and helps him to bear the ills of this life, because he considers them the necessary consequence of sins committed in an earlier life, and it is a strong spur to him to lead an honest life, every error in this life entailing an unavoidable penance in some future existence. Deeper contemplation, for which however, the present moment is not a suitable one, teaches us that the belief in the transmigration of souls is the allegorical expression of a truth that is unattainable for our conception, that it is truth in the garb of a myth. The truth proper, represented by this myth, we cannot realize owing to the organisation of our intellect, which is limited to time and space, and we should not even then be able to conceive it if an angel from heaven were to come to teach us.

The following evening we accepted an invitation to dine with Colonel M., in whose house we saw how English comfort has adapted itself to the conditions of Indian life, and where we met a small but select company of English guests. Colonel M. is one of those Englishmen—all too rare unfortunately—who do not speak ill of the natives, and of whom I am convinced the natives would have nothing bad to say. "I am in the habit of treating the Indians like children," he told me, "and have always got on very well with them." After dinner, the ladies having retired as usual to the drawing-room, and the gentlemen having lighted their cigars, the conversation turned upon an important question, the early native marriages. As is well known in most Indian castes the law prevails that all girls must be married before having completed their 11th year. On this account a father with a daughter begins betimes to look about him among the members of his caste, for there is no question of any other. He begins by cautiously throwing out feelers; negotiations between the two sets of parents are then entered into, the fortunes, suitability of character, &c., are carefully considered, and the union is then concluded by the parents, a union irrevocably binding the girl of eleven and the boy of about sixteen for the rest of their lives. The wedding is celebrated with great pomp and ceremony, of which we shall have more to say later on; the child-wife continues to live in the house of her parents and the boy-husband goes on attending school. If he behaves well, he is occasionally invited to dinner by his parents-in-law, when he has an opportunity of seeing his wife. The actual marriage only takes place on the girl's having attained maturity, when she is about fourteen. She is then handed over to her husband with renewed though less solemn ceremonies, and now lives with him in the house of the parents-in-law, it being quite customary for parents and married children to form one household in India.

There is much to be said both for and against these child-marriages. After all, the result of the matter is, that in India it is the parents who arrange the match, whereas the young couple acts more or less independently with us. When we consider the innumerable mistakes that attend on love-matches, mistakes having often to be atoned for by a life-time of misery, we may perhaps arrive at the conclusion that the Indian method is not so bad after all. To be sure the charm of falling in love, the longing and pining, are wanting, and such a love-drama as Shakuntalâ has ceased to be possible under existing circumstances in India. On the other hand, there is none of the unsatisfied longing, the feeling of despair that comes over our girls when they feel themselves growing older; none of the flirting, flattering and other artifices indulged in both by mothers and daughters to catch a husband by hook or by crook. There is no empty blank in the existence, such as so often falls to the lot of our old maids, for there are no old maids, and should there be more girls than there are husbands for, then men must take two wives, for all the girls must be disposed of. The great nuisance in India however is the case of the young widows. Should a girl of eleven marry and her young husband die, she is doomed to remain a widow for the rest of her life, is prohibited from marrying again, and is forced to lead a secluded and more or less joyless life in the house of her parents-in-law. The widower, on the contrary, may marry as often again as he pleases, only he has no other choice than to wed a girl of eleven, for there are no others to be had, even should he himself be sixty. The worst thing about these early marriages however is what was discussed that evening at Colonel M.'s. The actual married life begins too early for the girls, before their bodies have attained a sufficient power of resistance; the consequence is that not only do the women fade very quickly, pine away and die, but they bring very delicate children into the world, and this with the absence of animal food, is probably the chief reason why the Indian, though not less intelligent, is both physically and mentally unable to compete with a European. The less prejudiced natives are themselves convinced of the impropriety of early marriages, but as yet they have not been able to decide upon a remedy which will not entail other evils.

As in the other towns we paid a visit to the Sanskrit College of Jaipur. I found all teachers assembled, squatting on the ground, and, accustomed by this time to the habit, we took our places among them without ceremony on a cushion that was plentifully bespattered with ink. They put all sorts of questions about the Emperor William and Bismarck, about Germany and whether we had castes there, asking too if all Germans understood Sanskrit, and so on. I had to tell them all about my Professorship, my name, which was most felicitously rendered into Sanskrit as *Devasena*, my titles and so on. and was at last asked what caste I belonged to. I promptly gave the perfectly correct answer that I was a *Cûdra*, for according to the Brahmin system all foreigners are *Cûdras*, but reading amazement in the faces of my hearers I determined in future to adapt myself a little better to the opinions of those who put such questions. When asked subsequently about the caste I belonged to, a very frequent question, I used to answer that in my previous birth I had been a Brahman but that in consequence of some sin I had committed I had been compelled to be born again as a European, *i. e.*, a Cûdra, but that after studying the Veda and Vedanta, after coming to see India and sò many holy places and men I trusted I might be premitted to skip the intervening castes and return to the world the next time as a Brahmin. This fairy tale never failed to excite much merriment among my hearers, though on one occasion in Calcutta, it was taken up in all seriousness by a recluse, a female penitent, a story I shall refer to later on.

On the morning of the 5th of December we made our way to the station before 5 o'clock, in utter darkness. Here we had the pleasure of shaking hands once more with Colonel M. whom the inconvenience of the hour had not deterred from escorting a lady to the train, which was to take us in nine hours to Agra. Early rising when travelling is attended by numerous disagreeables, but it has its advantages too, especially in India, and particularly that very morning, for from the carriage windows we could watch the nocturnal darkness gradually turn to twilight and from twilight to dawn. I was forcibly reminded of the Hymn to the Dawn (Rig-Veda 6, 64,) the first Veda hymn I had read with Lassen in 1864, and the words of which had so often seemed to me to embody the spell the East has woven about us. How I really did see the waves of light turning from the faintest pink to a changing colour scheme of yellow and white, until the first rays of the sun shot up like lightning in the cloudless sky and a few minutes latter the fully risen orb of day was pouring down a flood of light upon all Nature, of which we under our leaden northern sky can form no conception. Our spirits rose too at the thought that we were now approaching the sacred *Yamuna,* which with its sister-river the Ganges, rouses such stirring memories, even though they appear to have been blotted out by the succeding Mahomedan epoch, just as in Italy the monuments of the Classic Ages were obliterated by the succeeding Christian Middle Ages.

About 2 o'clock, we reached Agra, which with Delhi forms the centre of the relics of the Mohammedan rule,and which is crowded with Mohammedan monuments. We sent our servant on to the hotel with our luggage and went straight from the station to the adjacent fort. From the Mohammedan mosques and palaces it contains, and which now serve the English for an arsenal, we had our first sight of the Yamuna, the widespread landscape on the other side of the river, and the world-famous Tâj-Mahal which lies about a quarter of an hour down the river. We were unable to resist the spell of this palace tomb, erected by Shah Jehan to his favourite consort Mumtax-i-Mahal (the Chosen One of the Palace); we recked little of the dusty road and the ardent afternoon sun; soon we had reached the temple-like entrance gate and there lay the magnificent Tâj-Mahal before us in the midst of its luxuriously verdant park. The overwhelming impression produced on the spectator, in spite of all the pictures he may have seen of it before, is mainly due to the effect of the contrast. The glittering channel of water with its lotus-flowers, extending from the entrance gate through the garden to the Tâj-Mahal itself, the proud pile of snow-white marble, the luxuriant green vegetation round about, and above the dark blue of the Indian sky, all combines to form a picture which for a moment banishes from the soul of the spectator all earthly cares and sorrows, and in its all-powerful effect may be held unrivalled in this world. On the other hand, I cannot agree with those who pronounce the Tâj-Mahal the finest specimen of architecture in the world. Those who have seen Cologne Cathedral, St Peter's in Rome, the beautiful Hagia Sophia in Constantinople (beautiful in the interior at all events) and, above all, the Parthenon in Athens, will not to able to look upon the Tâj-Mahal as the highest type of architectural beauty, notwithstanding the noble simplicity of its forms and proportions. The Mohammedan dome in particular can compete with the Romanic neither in form nor in its adjustment. The contraction the former shows at its base is thoroughly well motived it is true, it is intended to emphasize the enormous weight of the dome, just as in the Doric temple the weight of the arch is more forcibly impressed upon the spectator by the swelling of the capital. But whereas the Doric pillar offers a strong resistance to the pressure above it, the bend at the base of the Mohammedan dome gives one rather an idea of weakness.

The afternoon was passed in viewing these and other sights. The setting sun was already gilding the domes and minarets of the proud palace tomb with its last rays, when a well-dressed young man came up to us and addressed us by name. It was Lâl Baij Nâth, a Judge in Agra, who had been informed of our arrival by letter, and who after going to the hotel in vain quest of us, had been at no loss to know whither he should follow us. We sent our carriage on ahead and turned our steps citywards in the cool of the evening. Our conversation soon turned to things spiritual, and it seemed to me that my companion was inclined to adopt a somewhat haughty attitude. In his first answers I seemed to read thequestion how I a European had any right to have any say in the matter. A few explanations sufficed to bring about a change in his mental attitude; his warm interest kept increasing and he never wearied of putting fresh questions on the questions that attracted him. He took his Vedanta faith in all seriousness; his devotional book for every day was the voluminous *Yogavasishtha*, and he showed a certain inclination not to stop at the *Râja-Yoga*, the intelectual subjection to the divine, but to go on to the *Hatha-Yoga*, which aims at the complete extermination of worldliness by employlng more or less forcible methods. His tendencies were much the same as those of our own Pietists, in so far as we may define their character as not being satisfied with awaiting the moment of grace, but endeavouring to attain it by persistent exercises in penitence and conversion. The argument used by us against Pietism is that the re-birth is only then genuine if brought about by the Holy Ghost without intervention on our own part. I was able to make the young Indian understand this in his own language by pointing to certain passages of the Veda, in which we are told that the Atman only takes its place in the breast of the person it chooses, and that all works, both good and evil, are of no avail where it is a question of the Very Highest.

The days in Agra were principally spent in Lâl Baij Nâth's company. Early next morning he came to fetch us from the hotel in his carriage, and drove with us to *Sikandra*, about an hour's distance from Agra, to see the tomb of the Emperor Akbar. This too is a mighty palace with a number of towers, pillars, and entrances. There is a broad terrace on the roof which commands a magnificent view of the surrounding park and the broad Indian landscape. Nothing disturbed the perfect peace that reigned, but the sweet twittering of the pretty little green parrots, whole flocks of which perched in the tops of the huge trees around us. "I often come here," said Lâl Baij Nâth, "to indulge in contemplation," and, indeed, no more suitable spot can be imagined for self-communion than the great Indian Emperor's monument in its world-forgotten solitude. Our friend took us too to many a memorial site of the past Mohammedan splendor, not forgetting the town with its arts, and crafts, and shops. In the evening we went to our friend's house, which lay outside the town. He had asked me on this occasion to talk more freely and connectedly on the subject we had already discussed, and had asked permission to invite a few friends. I made no objections, but was not a little surprised to find a goodly audience assembled, so that my address took the form of a proper lecture on all the chief points of the Vedânta system. In the ensuing discussion, which was conducted partly in Sanskrit, partly in English, I was struck by the theistic tendency displayed, and which is peculiar to many of the Vedântists now-a-days, but of this we shall have to speak more fully later on. The friends present at this first and almost fortuitous lecture, must, I fancy, have spread the news of it either by letter or through the papers, if not by word of mouth. At several places I afterwards stopped at the fact was well known, and referring to it I was asked for a lecture, which I either gave or withheld according to the circumstances.

The company at Lâl Baij Nâth's having withdrawn, we were left alone with our host, who kept us to have dinner with him. "To-day," he said "you are to have a European meal, but to-morrow evening my wife is going to cook you a Hindu meal. I can only look on at to-night's dinner, but to-morrow evening, though my caste prescribes my remaining at a certain distance, I shall join you."

This occasion may be taken of giving a few details respecting the Hindu meals, which we had frequent opportunities of noting, both then and later. The orthodox Indian, as already prescribed in the Veda, takes two meals a day only, one in the morning at 11 o'clock, the other in the evening at 8. The food is prepared by the wife or wives, who generally serve their husband during the repast, though not of course when Europeans are present. Not till the men have finished their meal do the women sit down to table. The food is limited to milk and vegetables; meat, fish, even eggs are prohibited. Spirituous liquors are also forbidden, the orthodox Indian drinking nothing but pure water and milk; they even object to tea and lemonade. In an airy hall of the house square wooden boards resembling our drawing boards, and corresponding in number by the number of the guests, are placed before those who have come to dine, after a servant has first poured water over their hands and they have seated themselves cross-legged. The food is then placed before each of them on the board, in little clay dishes or on banana leaves. The number of the dishes is very great: twelve to twenty courses is nothing out of the way. The dishes mostly consist of various vegetables all very highly seasoned, of milk food, rice, stewed fruit, &c., &c., and nearly the half of them are sweetmeats. There is no bread, but in its stead so-called *Chapatis*, thin wafers baked in the pan, are placed in piles before each guest. They serve at the same time in place of spoons, to scoop up the half liquid milk food. Nothing in the way of knives or forks is used. You eat with your right hand, dipping at will into one or other of the little dishes, and carefully carrying the morsel chosen to the mouth. What is left over is never saved, but either given to the Mohammedans or *Çûdras*, if not thrown away. Everything put on the table has been freshly cooked that very day. The raw products being exceedingly cheap it is possible to have a very opulent meal for about two annas (two pence). At the conclusion of the meal water is again poured over the hands of the guest and the Tâmbûlam is then handed to him. It consists of a rolled-up betel-leaf, containing little pieces of areca-nut and other spices (Cardamom, cinnamon, and cloves). The little packet is pushed into the mouth and slowly allowed to dissolve, until the whole has been swallowed, many then partaking of a second dose. Many people, in fact, chew betel all day long. It is said to aid the digestion; in taste it is strong and spicy, but not disagreeable. For an Indian it takes the place of a cigar; the smoking of tobacco is but little practised, except among the Bengalees; most Indians abstain from it because it is not expressly permitted by the Veda, while the few who do smoke soothe their consciences with the reflection that neither does the Veda prohibit it. India, by the way, grows a great deal of tobacco, from which no very fine, but very tolerable middling cigars are manufactured. The best cost three, four, or at the most five rupees a hundred. The price after that at once rises to fifteen rupees and more for imported cigars. After dining the Indians are very fond of music, and so was Lâl Baij Bâth, who, squatting on the carpet, with his back comfortably leant against a big cushion sang us a few songs on both occasions, accompanying himself on the lute.

When we said good-bye in the evening Lâl Baij Nâth presented me with an ebony stick as a keepsake

It was entirely covered with beautiful carving and encrusted with precious stones, and was an antique object he had picked up at an auction in Benares. An Arabian name is engraved on the handle in curiously intertwined characters in inlaid ivory. My friend and colleague Hoffmann has made them out to be *Osman Elias Muhammed Padischah*, and, judging by the last title, assumes the stick to have once been the property of an Indian Emperor. In the course of time it must have passed through many hands before reaching those of its present owner, who will take good care not to let it pass out of them. I managed to bring it safely home after all the vicissitudes of our journey, and I cherish it as a souvenir not only of the donor, of the days spent in Agra, but of the magnificent country that lives in our memory as a lost paradise.

Meanwhile the 8th of December had come and winter was beginning to make itself felt, so that the Hindus could be seen cowering morning and evening about their tiny fires, either outside their houses or inside, where however owing to the absence of chimneys the smoke makes its way out as best it can at doors and windows, as well as through the chinks it finds in the thatched or tiled roofs. The fuel is still the same we find mentioned in the Rig-Veda, *i.e.*, cow-dung, which is carefully gathered up, shaped into little cakes and plastered on the outside walls of the huts to dry in the sun. In burning it emits a peculiar penetrating smell of ammonia; were I ever to smell it again it would at once transport me back to India.

The approaching winter reminded us too not to put off our excursion to the far North any longer, *i. e.*, to the Punjab, the most ancient seat of Indian culture. We decided to leave Delhi and everything else till our return, and to go straight from Agra *via* Lahore to Peshawar, the North-western terminus of the Anglo-Indian Empire.

In the morning of December the 8th we bade Lâl Baij Nâth and the fair city of Agra a hearty farewell, to set out on our twenty-two hours of railway travelling to Lahore, the capital of the Punjab. The Punjab, which lies in the North-west of the Indian Empire, and is seldom visited by the average traveller, was of particular interest to me, being the seat of the most ancient Indian culture, of which we have such vivid pictures in the hymns of the Rig-Veda, pictures which have lost none of their brightness and colouring, despite the lapse of three to four thousand years. Since then, to be sure, one race after the other has surged across the Punjab; here Alexander's invasions brought Greek culture in its train; here again the Mohammedans broke in, and here they still maintain their ascendancy, the half, if not more, of the population in the North-west being Mohammedan. These Mohammedans, it must be owned, are but Arabian immigrants in a certain degree only; a great number of them are Hindus who have been converted to Islam, and it would be exceedingly interesting, especially for the appreciation of the influence exercised upon humanity by religion, to ascertain whether the islamitized Hindus are more Hindu or more Mohammedan, the difference between the two being vast. The chief traits of the Mohammedan character may be said to be fanaticism, a tendency to violence, and greed. Anyone who has ever been in Egypt or Palestine will have a lively recollection of the shameless begging, the eternal whining for *bakscheesh* and the discontent with which the most munificent alms is wont to be received. The Mohammedans in India display similar traits, though not in so pronounced a degree. Yet in spite of their greed they have no proper money-making impulses and in this way they differ widely from their first-cousins, the Jews. The Jew is inspired by the love of gain too, but he is at the same time thrifty and sober, and in consequence often succeeds in acquiring a fortune which is almost awe-inspiring for his Christian fellow-citizens. The Mohammedan in India on the other hand, as I was repeatedly told, only hoards, to be able to waste what he has acquired. He therefore seldom succeeds in gaining a large fortune and a correspondingly influential position in society. The Mohammedan, owing to the absence of all caste prejudices, is better adapted to act as a servant than the Hindu. The cooks in the hotels and Dak bungalows are nearly all Mohammedans. The strong sensuality of the race is a familiar fact. One consequence of it is the rigid seclusion in which their women are kept, and nothing more comical can be imagined than a Mohammedan travelling with the women of his harem. On getting out of the compartment each of the women has at once to slip into a scrupulously closed litter, in which she is carried to the carriage. Failing a litter the husband pulls a long sack over each of his wives in succession. This sack covers her to the very feet, and the husband hurries her to a remote corner of the station, where she either stands or squats motionless until the debarcation of all the immates of the harem has been performed in the same fashion, when they are all transferred to a carriage. We had frequent opportunities of noting such and similar scenes on our journey north. We reached Umballa four hours after leaving Agra, and eight hours more of a night journey took us to Lahore, where we arrived at 7 o'clock on the next morning.

Intending to continue our journey the same evening we left our luggage at the station in charge of our servant, and went for a morning walk through the town. We had seen a model of Lahore in the India Museum in London, which it must be admitted gives a very good idea of the plan on which Indian cities are built.

Generally speaking the Indian city may be compared with a circle, with a tangent attached to it. The surface of the circle is formed by the narrow native town with its winding crooked angular lanes, the tangent consisting of a fine broad street generally termed The Mall, round which cross and parallel streets have grouped themselves, all very wide, straight and well-kept. This is the European quarter, which not infrequently is divided into Civil Lines and the

Cantonment. The latter portion is properly reserved for the officers, but a number of civil residences are met with here too. The broad roads we have mentioned, which extend for miles and lend the town a circumference that calls for a carriage, are not bordered by houses, but by large properties with fine gardens and parks, in the midst of which, at a considerable distance from the road and each other stand large villas, and palatial residences with colonnades and fine halls. Some of these are private residences others again are hotels, banks, warehouses, &c. The European tradesmen too, appear to live very comfortably in India. In Lahore I happened to be sitting in the hotel one evening after dinner, smoking my cigar in front of a fire which the evening air rendered most grateful, and talking to some gentlemen. One of them, who was both well-dressed and well-bred, seemed to be exceedingly well-informed about matters, and I was not a little surprised to learn in the course of our conversation that he was merely the Army tailor.

The morning of our arrival we walked through the roads and gardens of the European quarter to reach the native town, in the narrow streets of which a crowd of people was surging, most of the houses opening into shops on the side of the street. Here the most multifarious products were being offered for sale in sacks, barrels and boxes, the salesmen gravely and quietly squatting behind them.

Having tasted to the full the pleasure of losing one's way and finding it again in the labyrinth of streets, I was seized with a desire to see the river on which Lahore lies. It is the Râvi, as it is now called, the Irâvatî of the Rig Veda (the Thirst Quencher), the middle river of the five tributaries of the Indus, which have given the Punjaub its name. In the rainy season Indian rivers are apt to change their beds; even the Ganges ploughs new ways for itself, occasioning the owners of the adjacent fields frequent differences of opinion, and much hard work. So it happens that nowadays the Irâvatî flows at about a quarter of an hour's distance from Lahore. We found a boy on his way back from school with his Sanscrit primer and to his delight we took a carriage and let him get in with us. We had soon left the town behind us, our way led through fields and waste lands, and soon the river was reached. We crossed it by a pontoon bridge, extremely primitive, as these bridges often are in India, and had a good view of the landscape. The charm of the southern vegetation was not so striking, as the surrounding country like the greater part of Hindustan is a perfectly flat plain, the mighty masses of the Himâlayas being too far off to be visible to the naked eye. We drove back to the town somewhat disappointed, stopped at a school and got the teacher to take us to the President of the Arya Samâj, a religious association, branches of which are found all over India, its chief seat however being in Lahore.

Several such associations have been formed in India in recent years; they all emanate from the desire to revive older and more worthy views in the degenerate popular religion, which has degenerated into a mere outward dead ceremony. The Brahma Samâj has adopted a number of foreign, and in particular of Christian elements, the Dharma Samâj goes to the opposite extreme and even tolerates idolatry, but the Arya Samâj, the most widely spread association, and the one with the most prospects for the future, has chosen the golden mean between the two. Though studiously keeping everything foreign at arm's length, it at the same time condemns the worship of idols and aspires to a return to the religion of the Veda. This tendency is widely spread among the Hindus who think, and if at the ticket-office window at the railway station a clerk is seen, whose eyes, behind the almost universal spectacles, express benevolence, and whose face bears a look of contemplation, you will not be far wrong in putting him down as a member of the Arya Samâj, and if you address him as such, the most friendly terms are speedily arrived at. In the larger towns the Arya Samaj has a house of its own in which a kind of regular divine service is held. It contains no idols, but in the middle of it, in a little square space about the size of a chimney opening, a fire is kept burning. I have been in one of these halls, but though cordially invited to be present, had never an opportunity of going to a service. After what I have heard, hymns from the Veda, passages from the Upanishads, are read aloud, on which a sermon is then preached. In Lahore a certain Hans Raj, still young in years, of pleasant appearance and unassuming manners, happens to be at the head of the Arya Samâj, and with him I had a short interview. He enjoys a very great esteem, having given up everything in order to place himself at the service of the Arya Samâj entirely without remuneration. I left Hans Raj and got someone to take me to Doctor Stein, a young but most meritorious Sanscrit scholar, at that time Principal of the Sanscrit College in Lahore. He received us most kindly and, with a certain amiable jealousy, tore us from the Arya Samâj folk to take entire possession of us himself. We had to breakfast with him then and there, and drink a bottle of perfectly excellent Cashmere wine. Our friend Stein had no very exalted opinion of India, but he was all the more enthusiastic about Cashmere, in which he has made extensive travels, and diligent researches for the publication of his edition of the Râjatarnaginî. He told us a great deal about the beauty of this mountain kingdom and of the primitive fashion of travelling there, the only bridges across streams for instance being three ropes, one to walk on, while you hold on to the two others with your hands.

We spent the day most pleasantly in the company of Doctor Stein, who was excellently versed in everything and showed us various of the town sights. After having dined with him in the hotel, and promising to spend a few days in Lahore on our return, we got into the night train, which had taken us to Rawal Pindi by the time we woke next morning. Numerous soldiers at the station and the quantity of military buildings and erections in the neighbourhood testified that the English had a strong fort here. After an excellent breakfast, more excellent than is usually to be met with at the stations, we continued our journey, and by noon had reached the Indus at the point where the Cabul river flows into it from the west, while east of the river, Attock, which is strongly fortified, nestles picturesquely at the foot of the mountain slopes. A magnificent railway-bridge spans the Indus, which here flows placidly with mountains on either hand, in no way however realizing one's idea of a mighty stream. As I remember it it was scarcely bigger than the Rhine at Bâle. In the rainy season, when the water rushes down into it on all sides from the mountains it may assume another aspect. The railway now extends westwards through the Cabul valley plain, which is shut in on all sides by mountains, till it reaches the terminus at Peshawar. Here we arrived in the course of the afternoon, and at once went to the only hotel in the place. We should have done better to choose the Dak Bungalow; the very first glance showed us that this hotel, the worst we chanced upon in India, was in a state of complete neglect. There were no other visitors beside ourselves, and the visitors' book proved that strangers had appeared but rarely, to disappear with all haste. An old woman introduced herself as the owner of the hotel; she showed us into a very primitive room, and to my no small astonishment demanded six rupees per day and per person, whereas with three established exceptions we had only paid five rupees everywhere else in the best hotels. On my drawing her attention to this she at once reduced her charges to five rupees, but afterwards tried to cheat us again by putting the dinner in the bill as an extra, on the monstrous pretext that board did not include dinner. Of course she did not get her own way in this, so she was reduced to overcharging us to the best of her ability in all the trifles it was not worth bargaining about. We went into the so-called drawingroom, in which all sorts of domestic utensils were curiously assorted, and the evening being cool I spent a good time in trying to fan the scanty fire into a proper flame with a broken bellows, but in vain.

Meantime we had sent a letter to Colonel Y., the chief personage in Peshawar, with a request to be allowed to visit Fort Jamrud. Jamrud lies about two hours' distance west of Peshawar, where the Indian plain comes to its very end, and the great road winds its way up through the celebrated Khaiber Pass into the mountains leading to Cabul in Afghanistan. Here the British rule comes to an end too, thanks to whose authority we were enabled to travel in India, just as securely as if we had been at home in Germany. On the other side of Fort Jamrud it is a different story. The English sphere of influence ceases, but between the English territory and Afghanistan there is a neutral strip of land about thirteen miles in breadth, inhabited by the so-called independent tribes. Jealous as these are of their independence, their lot is but little enviable. General anarchy is the consequence, and in the various villages the parties stand to each other much as the Montagues and Capulets did in Shakespere's "Romeo and Juliet." There is no such thing as public safety and welfare; every one carries arms, and quarrels and bloodshed are never-ending. No stranger can set foot on this territory without running the risk of being looked upon as a spy and shot down at a moment's notice. From time to time such an accident takes place, whereupon the English burn down a few villages in return. To prevent such occurrences the English Government allows nobody to set foot on the Khaiber Pass except on Tuesdays and Fridays, when the Pass is open, and a sufficient garrison of soldiers guarantees the security of caravans and travellers.

To see these things close at hand we needed a pass from Colonel Y. and for this purpose I had sent a letter from our hotel to his house in Peshawar. The messenger came back with the news that the Colonel was at Fort Jamrud, so we decided to go and find him there the following morning.

It was on a perfectly lovely Sunday morning that we set out. The sun was blazing down in all its splendour on the Cabul River plain, which was thrown into striking relief by the lofty blue mountains skirting it. Owing to the northern latitude as well as to the vicinity of the mountains, the air was fresh and cool as we were trundled along Jamrudwards in a *tam-tam* (a light two-wheeled vehicle accommodating three inmates and the coachman, who are seated back to back.) The vegetation in the Cabul Valley was particularly fine this winter owing, as we learned, to the unusually plentiful rains, which, it is true, brought more fever than usual in their train. We kept getting closer to the mountains, and it was with a certain pleasure that we estimated that we had reached the point in India nearest the latitude of our own home. From a practical stand-point we were actually further from it than anywhere else. For what an undertaking would it have been to attempt a return home by making a bee-line across Afghanistan, Persia and Turkish Asia Minor or Russia. Yet the English and Russian railway networks are gradually approaching, and the time is none too far off when, in spite of all political and technical difficulties, they will at last join, and it will then be possible to travel by rail straight from Berlin to Calcutta in about ten days and nights. Indulging in these and other day dreams we had got to the foot of the lowering mountain ridge, and there on a hill to the left lay Jamrud, the first village beyond the British frontier, while opposite it on the right or English side, lies the small but very respectably fortified Fort Jamrud. Between the two places the road wound its way up the thickly wooded mountain slope to the Khaiber Pass. We stopped in front of the Fort and sent in our cards to Colonel Y. He welcomed us warmly in his study, where he was consulting with a native Colonel whom he introduced to us, but whose name has unfortunately slipped my memory. A native Colonel! Surely a very rare thing for a native to attain so high a rank in India. Exceptional circumstances too have led to his advancement. The man belonged to the district, and had acquired such an authority over the natives, thanks to his eminent parts, that the English were glad to be able to give the English General the support of an energetic personality, familiar with the language, land and people, more especially so in such a frontier station where countless complications are all too apt to arise with which an Englishman would be perfectly unable to cope. The man's personal appearance bore this out; he spoke next to no English, but his tall powerful figure inspired respect, his eye betokened courage and a clear understanding, his features expressed a resolution and energy that would brook no insubordination, and would carry all before him.

After he had shaken hands with and said good-bye to us Colonel Y. gave us a picture of the existing state of affairs, entirely corroborating what we had already heard and noted. "You cannot set foot on the Khaiber Pass," he said, "except on Tuesdays and Fridays, without risking your lives; I should not even advise you to pay a visit to the village of Jamrud; you would see nothing there but what you have already seen elsewhere, and the inhabitants are not fond of foreigners; being Mahomedans they are very jealous of their women and they all carry arms. On the other hand, immediately in front of the village there is a pond that still bears the name of the pond of *Jemschid.* Professor Darmesteter has found a trace of the Iranian legend in this. Should you desire to see it I will give you an escort to it." We gratefully accepted the offer; ten soldiers, all of them brown-skinned Hindus, marched up, gun on shoulder, and escorted us to the pond, which was nearly dry. From it we had a good view of the principal village street, the people sitting about in it and the men walking about with their muskets. Contenting ourselves with this glimpse of the prevailing disorder of the Iranian frontier we retraced our steps, chatting with a Hindu who could speak English, and whom the Colonel had sent with us. At first he was exceedingly reserved, but grew warm and communicative when we mentioned our connection with the Arya Samâj, to which he belonged. It was his office to collect the customary toll from the caravans—two rupees per camel.

After having partaken of the lunch we had brought with us, inside the Fort, in the shade of our carriage, we set off back again. Our rapid drive was suddenly brought to an abrupt halt, our driver pulling up in front of a tiny house by the roadside, where a native was seated smoking his hookah (an Indian pipe.) Our coachman sprang from his seat, requested the smoker to lend him his pipe, indulged in two or three vigorous puffs, and, thus refreshed, jumped up to his box again. We now drove briskly on, and at about half past two had reached our hotel again. Here a young Hindu had meantime turned up, who had been written to of our intended arrival. He was a kind and gentle youth in delicate health, in fact he appeared to be consumptive. He was a student of philosophy, and complained bitterly that the English professors of philosophy had almost spoiled his pleasure in it. I could the more readily understand these complaints, as somewhat the same state of things prevails with us. What pleases to term itself philosophy here, at home in Germany, in England, and—as far as English influence extends—in India, is no longer the science of Plato and Aristotle, but a psychological system of experimenting, the actual value of which is decidedly questionable, and which, in the best of cases, may be looked upon as ante-room into the halls of philosophy, though it now presumes to oust true philosophy and to usurp its place. I drew the young man's attention to the native philosophy of the Vedanta, and the treasures of thought which it contains; the little I was able to say in the limited time seemed to inspire him with fresh courage. He showed great fondness for our society and took a walk with us through the town. The bazaar, to which we first paid a visit, was particularly interesting, not only on account of the wares coming from the mountains beyond the frontier, but also on account of the half-savage mountaineers, dressed in skins, who had come down to exchange the raw products of their district for the products of civilisation. "Do you see these figures?" said our companion, pointing to a group, romantically accoutred in sheepskins, "they belong to the independent tribes beyond the frontier; when they come here to dispose of their sheepskins and cheeses they are tame enough, but I have no wish to meet with them over yonder in the mountains." From the bazaar our young friend took us up to the flat roof of one of the public buildings, and from there we had a fine view over the whole town. Everywhere smoke was rising from the streets and the roofs of the houses. It came from the fires that had been lit as the air grew more chilly with the gathering night. Peshawar is notorious for its frequent fires, and it is easy to understand how they happen so often. In the street in front of a house I myself saw a fire, the blazing flames of which were quite close to the woodwork of the balustrade and gable. Evening was approaching, and with it the hour of our intended departure. We had a long journey to Lahore before us and I had been cautious enough to have the two under berths of a first class compartment reserved, trusting that we should have the compartment to ourselves as usual. But as it chanced, things were to turn out differently.

CHAPTER V.

From Peshawar to Calcutta.

THE OBLIGING Hindu youth, who had been so good a guide to us in Peshawar, was not to be dissuaded from seeing us off at the station. He helped us into our compartment, presenting us with a number of boxes of most delightful grapes for our refreshment on the way, bade us a hearty good-bye, and our train moved away. We had the compartment to ourselves and hoped to sleep soundly while passing through the Indus Valley which we had already travelled through by day, in order the better to enjoy our next day's journey along the five eastern tributaries, from which the Punjab takes its name. We undressed and lay down to sleep; the train stopped at the next station, the door of the compartment was opened and in got a lady and a gentleman. It was most annoying, but there was no help for it. The two upper berths were let down, and our two companions climbed up into them. It was some small comfort to learn that they intended getting out at Rawal Pindi at three o'clock in the morning, but till then sleep was out of the question. True, our companions up above were considerately quiet, but actuated by the very justifiable desire not to miss their station they could not refrain from letting down the window at a station from time to time and inquiring where we were, or from occasionally lighting a match to see what time it was. At last Rawal Pindi came, and we had our quarters to ourselves again. But at the very next station in got two sportsmen and took possession of the upper beds. The morning after this broken night's rest we reached *Jhelum*, lying on the first of the eastern tributaries of the Indus; this tributary still bears the name of the *Jhelum*, though by the Greeks it was called the *Hydaspes*, and in the Veda the *Vitastâ*, *i.e.*, the wide-spread one. Nor does it belie its name, a seemingly never-ending railway bridge spanning the numerous water-courses into which it resolves itself during the dry season. During the rainy season they all unite to form one stream of water, I suppose, and it must be a majestic sight, more especially as here the panorama is bounded on the north by the spurs of the Himâlayas, in which these mighty waters take their rise. The railway now crosses the *Doab*, between the Jhelum and the Chenab. In the Punjaub the name of Doab is used to signify the table-lands situated between two rivers, and which in some parts present a somewhat barren appearance. Altogether the Punjaub does not come up to the idea we form of it from the Rig Veda, a land fertile in woods and grassy lawns, so little so indeed that Doctor Stein hazarded the opinion that the Indians of the Rig Veda may probably have had their home in the northern mountain territory. The facts, however, contradict this theory. For instance, when in the well-known hymn to the rivers (Rig Veda 3, 33) *Viswâmitra* sings the praises of the *Vipâs* and the *Sutudri*, this song can scarcely have been composed anywhere but at the juncture of the *Bias* and the *Sutlej* to the south of *Amritsar*, where the mountains are at more than seventy miles distance. We must therefore rather conclude that in consequence of the extensive deforestation, the soil has become so very dry. The influence this may have upon a climate is to be seen in Greece and Palestine, where the bare arid mountains in no way correspond to the scenery described in the Bible and the Classics. In the Punjaub the Arabs have played the part that the Turks enacted in Greece and Palestine. Both races are prone to live without taking thought for the morrow, leaving the cares for the future to Allah. We then crossed the Chenab, the ancient Candrabhâgâ, and got safely back to Lahore at about four o'clock in the afternoon. At the station a Pandit was already waiting to welcome us, and with him I strolled to the hotel on foot, where Doctor Stein soon put in an appearance, his place being taken later in the evening by several Pandits. Our talk turned on astronomy, and to my amazement I observed that these learned men, being restricted to their ancient native books of science, still made the heavens with all their suns, revolve round our little earth with inconceivable rapidity within twenty-four hours. The starry firmament above us had led up to the conversation, and here, as so often in India, I was struck with the difference between it and our northern sky. The Great Bear stands so low on the horizon that, as a rule, it can scarcely be made out, being either entirely or partially obscured by the vapours of the horizon, if it does not chance to be entirely below it. The Pole Star is not easy to make out either for the same reasons, and once found, its position low down on the horizon arouses the same astonishment.

Having four nights behind us, three of which had been spent in the train and under trying circumstances we went to bed early. On the following days Doctor Stein used to fetch us at seven o'clock to take a bracing morning walk. We went to see the gardens with their interesting but miserably kept beasts; the simple stone monuments the Indians were in the habit of erecting on the spot where a widow had been burned alive with her husband's corpse; the water-wheels and other arrangements for irrigating the land. We then generally went to see our friend in his Sanscrit College. To my delight I saw that he was reading the hymns of the Rig Veda with his Hindu students. This is the more especially meritorious as the natives happen rather to neglect the Rig Veda. Nor do I know in what other part of the world these most ancient monuments of Indian culture more thoroughly deserve to be read, if not in the country where they were first sung, on the banks of the Irâvatî. Under Doctor Stein's supervision quite a number of excellent Pandits lecture, and I attended their lectures with great pleasure. I made closer acquaintance of one other Pandit, who teaches

Sanscrit in a Mission Institute. He had a great mind to come to Europe and made most minute inquiries as to whether it would be possible for him to earn his living by giving Sanscrit lectures. To my regret I had to assure him that there was not the slightest prospect of that, either now or in the immediate future, for are we not entering upon an era when even the knowledge of Greek is about to be confined to a privileged few? We were forcibly reminded of Greece in Lahore, when we went to the Museum there with Doctor Stein. The sculptures it contains undoubtedly betray Greek influences, and form therefore a striking contrast to the specimens of purely native plastic.

A few days were passed most pleasantly in seeing the sights of the town and the vicinity. Under these circumstances it was, however, not quite so easy to get into closer touch with the Arya Samâj Association. They asked me to give a lecture, to which I readily agreed, but owing to some misunderstanding no preparations had been made for the evening fixed upon. There was but a small audience of members who had been hastily summoned, and I confined myself to giving them a short address. All the more numerous were the gifts of books which I got when we came to say good-bye. They were mostly editions of the more familiar Upanishads, with explanations and English translations, which, however, do not give one a very high opinion of the state of the exegesis of the Veda, which would appear to be very primitive.

On the afternoon of December the 14th, we left Lahore to proceed to Amritsar, a very short railway journey. The famous so-called Golden Temple in this town makes it well worth the traveller's while to break his journey here, in spite of the night's having to be spent in a very mediocre Dak Bungalow. After depositing our things there we drove at once, for evening was at hand, to the Golden Temple, which belongs to the Sikhs, whose religion is a mixture of Hindu and Mahomedan elements, Amritsar being its chief seat. The Temple is not large, but is beautifully situated in the heart of the town, in the middle of a big pond, in which its golden domes are reflected. It is reached by a long bridge, on which at the hour of our arrival an amazing mass of humanity was surging up and down. Every stranger has to have a pair of sandals tied on by one or other of the obsequious boys always on the look-out for a tip, nor is the stranger admitted unless under the escort of a native policeman, something quite unusual in India, and which is here due to the strong fanaticism that prevails. The inside of the Temple, filled with a motley crowd of worshippers, we were not of course allowed to penetrate into, but we had a perfectly adequate view of it through the wide-open door. A guide conducts strangers to the flat roof, which permits a close view of the gilded copper slabs with which the domes and other portions of the Temple are covered, and from which the Temple takes its name. The falling night warned us to turn our steps Dak-wards. We had to pass through a maze of densely populated streets. The impudent forwardness of the hawkers, who did their best to stop the carriage whenever they could, gave proof of a constant stream of foreign visitors. There were very few guests in the Dak Bungalow, and we got into very pleasant conversation with them, especially with a Mr. Summers, a man in the prime of life, who turned out to be a Member of Parliament, and whose interested questions proved him to be far superior to the average Englishman. We sat with him till a late hour, and met him again on several occasions, in Delhi for instance, where he was inspecting schools with great zeal, and at Lucknow on Christmas Eve, when to dispel the antics of a band of Scotch musicians I played him some German Christmas carols. It was to be a last good-bye. Next day he set off for Allahabad to attend the National Congress, and two days later we heard that he was dangerously ill there, of what disease we did not hear. A few days later we read the notice of his death in the papers. When we came to Allahabad later we learned the details of his death in the hotel in which he had died. He had been seized by small-pox, and it was impressed upon us that in Parliament he had always been very strongly against compulsory vaccination.

We had neglected to have ourselves revaccinated before starting for India, and luckily we had no evil consequences to chronicle; but as matters lie, anyone travelling to India would do well not to omit this precautionary measure. Cholera, as we have already mentioned, does not attack a gentleman, to quote the

Hindu saying; fever chiefly prevails during the rainy season, but small-pox is a permanent danger, the traveller running the risk of infection from every bed or railway carriage a small-pox patient may have occupied.

Having said good-bye to Mr. Summers and the rest of the company in Amritsar that evening, we retired to our bedroom, and finding the door to be entirely destitute of lock or bolt, we had to barricade it as best we could by piling up our boxes and baggage. Dawn found us back at the station to begin a long railway journey that was to land us at Delhi after ten o'clock at night. Many a spot famous in tale and verse flashed past us. We first crossed the *Vipâs* (the unfettered) and the *Sutudri* (the hundred-currented), characteristic names which have since been changed to the *Bias* and the *Sutlej*. We crossed them a little above the point at which they meet, the spot at which more than three thousand years ago Viswâmitra was inspired to indite that song in the Rig Veda already mentioned, a song which strikes us as vividly as if it had been written but yesterday, and which conjures up for us across the ages a remote and ancient past. Farther on we crossed the tiny *Saraswatî*, the subject of so many lofty verses, though now it makes haste to vanish in the desert, and leaving the legend of the Rig Veda behind us we entered upon the scenes described in the *Mahâbhâratam*, skirting at *Karnal* station the district in which tradition places the great battle field. Late in the evening we reached Delhi, the capital of the great

Mogul Empire, built near the site of the ancient *Indraprastham*, the residence of the heroes of the *Mahâbhâratam*.

Delhi has very aptly been compared with Rome. Like Rome, Delhi has become in our days a busy centre of commerce, with this exception that whilst in Rome the toga and the tunic have made way for coat and trousers, Delhi, like the rest of India, has retained her ancient and picturesque costumes. As in Rome the monuments of the Papal dominion are everywhere met with, so in Delhi you meet with the no less magnificent remains of the Mahomedan glory. In Rome churches and chapels have intrusively planted themselves upon the relics of the classic past, and in Delhi the Mahomedan mosques, palaces and tombs have usurped the sites of an older and more interesting past, the relics of *Indraprastham*, the capital of the *Mahâbhârata* heroes. But whereas modern Rome is built immediately upon the site of the antique city, the ramparts at least of the ancient *Indraprastham* have been preserved to the south of Delhi. Just as to the south of Rome the Campagna extends with its numerous relics of classical antiquity, a district stretches two hours' distance to the south of Delhi, situated as far as *Kutb Minar*, with monuments of the Mahomedan period, as well as with some belonging to the ancient Indian period. As a description of all these splendours may be read elsewhere we must confine ourselves to chronicling a few personal impressions. We were provided with introductions to people in Delhi also, and they procured us an entrance into native circles. This time our arrival had been notified by letter to some rich merchants, and they appeared at our hotel the very next morning after our arrival to welcome us. With them we took a stroll through the park, lying within the city walls, to the south of the station, took a cursory glance at the Museum in it and then turned our steps to the *Chandni Chauk* (Silver Street), a street of no mean breadth, running the whole length of the town, which with its handsome shops and crowded traffic is ample testimony to the fact that here we have one of the industrial and commercial centres of India. We were much interested in a visit we paid with our friends to their warehouse. As is usual in India the house was built round a central closed court; it serves as a kind of reception-room, and in it business is conducted. Round it lies the house proper, provided with verandahs for every story, opening on to open arcades adjoining the court, the multifarious wares being stored in the interior. Like most merchants in India, where culture has not yet soared to the conception of a division of labour, our friends were General Merchants, *i. e.*, they not only exported, but imported and sold all sorts of articles. Our interests differed, however, too widely to admit of our becoming more intimate.

The chief street, Chandni Chauk, which runs from east to west cutting Delhi in two parts, ends at the eastern extremity in the Fort, magnificently situated on an eminence between the town and the *Yamunâ*;

it contains a number of exceedingly interesting halls and palatial buildings, and at the time of the Mahomedan dominion must have been fairy-like in its splendour, whereas nowadays the military purposes to which many of the buildings have been put, the pyramid-shaped piles of cannon-balls, the cannon on the ramparts, and the pacing sentinels, form a strange contrast to those monuments of the Great Mogul that have been left standing. The most remarkable of them are the magnificent general audience-hall (*Diwan-i-Am*) open on three sides, and the still finer private audience-hall (*Diwan-i-Khas*), lying nearer the Yamunâ, in the heart of the beautiful garden. With its wealth of marble and gold-fretted pillars and with the charming scenery in which it stands, it may well be said to deserve the Persian description that flaunts upon the walls.

> Should Earth still boast a second Paradise,
> What better site can mind surmise?

The terrible fate of Shah Jehan proves too well that earth boasts of no Paradise; all these splendours did not avail to save him from being betrayed by his own sons, who went to war against him, and having to end his life in prison.

Not far from the *Diwan-i-Khas*, and on the same slope that descends to the Yamunâ lies the costly though small *Moti-Musjid*, *i.e.*, the Pearl Mosque, built of white and grey marble. In its kind it is a pearl, and both its name and architecture testify to that fusion of the Indian and Islamitic elements which characterized the age it dates from.

Next to the Fort and all appertaining to it, the most magnificent building in Delhi is the *Jumma-Musjid*; it lies high and was completed in the year 1658, the very year in which that gloomy fanatic Aurungzeb usurped his father Shah Jehan's throne. Magnificent flights of steps lead up on three sides to a great square, framed in by walls and turrets, while on the fourth rises the mosque itself, consisting of an open, covered hall. In one of the little corner towers on the square in front a few precious relics are still shown; a slipper of the Prophet's and a hair from his beard, as well as the impression of his foot in stone, no very conclusive proof of the genuineness of the two other articles. Some old manuscripts of the Koran were vastly more interesting, one in particular from the time of Ali, 600 B. C.

We twice spent a day in Delhi sight-seeing in the district to the south of the town, a district rich in tombs, which are in a state of good preservation, and other monuments. On one occasion we were accompanied by one of the young merchants of our acquaintance, another time by a teacher whom we had got to know at his school, and whom we happened to pick up in the streets with his dog. At Humayun's grave, where he was refused admittance we lost the cur, to the teacher's great annoyance. At last, after long and vain whistling, hunting and searching, we set out on our way home, to find our doggy calmly awaiting us by the roadside on a heap of stones in the shade of a mango tree. We took it into the carriage and the troubled spirits were at last at rest.

We met with such a host of remarkable objects in the course of our perambulations to the south of Delhi, that we must limit ourselves to the mention of a very few. Immediately after having left Delhi by one of the southern gates, the eye, after wandering over a waste of ruins, falls upon the pillar of *Asoka* in the middle of what is now but a lofty pile of stones, but which was once the Fort of *Ferozabad*. The pillar, which was removed to its present site in the sixteenth century was erected together with a number of similar pillars by King *Asoka* in the year 250 B. C. and still bears on the upper portion the celebrated Pali inscription, as well as other inscriptions which were subsequently added. The inscription contains an edict of King *Asoka's* and is looked upon as the most ancient inscriptive monument in India. Still more ancient memories however are called forth by the *Purâna Qila* (the Old Fort) which lies farther to the south and which is also called *Indrapat*, thus designating the spot on which stood the city of the ancient Bharata King, *Yudhishtira*. It consists of a hill, surrounded by a very ancient, though mostly well-preserved wall, a Hindu village having snugly ensconced itself within. The entrance strongly reminds one of the Porta Marina, through which admittance is obtained to the excavations of Pompeii. Every time I ever visited Pompeii my imagination always set to work to repicture the streets and houses as they had used to be, and to repeople them with the figures of ancient Romans. What the imagination had but imperfectly succeeded in accomplishing there *Indraprastham* may be said to have realized to a certain extent. It was as if ancient Pompeii had come to life again—for scarcely had we passed through the gateway that reminded us of the Porta Marina, when on our left we saw a shoemaker in apron and turban squatting at his work; on our right, leaning against a pillar, were two figures who, but for their dark-skinned complexions, might have stepped out of the classic past. In the huts and shops, which were all open to the street, children either stark naked or half naked, were at play, and when we were met by two men naked to the loins carrying on their shoulders a pole from which a big clay vessel was hung, exactly as is so often to be seen upon ancient vases, the illusion was almost complete, and our delight was great. With the teacher above-mentioned we climbed to the top of an ancient tower which gave us a view of the whole village, affording us a convenient glimpse into the inner courts and rooms of the huts. Such a dwelling house usually consisted of a small square court shut in on all sides, a gate-like entrance occupied the front of the building. Opposite it was a roofed-in-hall, opening on to the court, and here the inmates of the house lived and had their being. In one corner there was a cooking-hearth; right and left of the court there were tiny stall-like spaces, all of which could be shut up, and which served as sleeping-rooms, for the men on one side, for the women on the other. After having inspected one of these houses more closely, and gratified the lady of the establishment by the gift of a few copper coins, we took a glance at the unimportant mosque and then went for a walk round the outskirts of the town, reverently admiring the lofty city walls, which must surely date, in part at least, from days of yore, and are in a state of good preservation.

A particularly fine sight is the *Kutb Minar*, about two hours' distance south of Delhi. It has a mighty tower five stories high and a mosque, partly constructed from the pillars and other remains of Hindu temples. In the middle of the court stands an exceedingly curious pillar, the wrought iron shaft of which, soaring to a height of twenty-three feet, glorifies in its Sanscrit inscription the victory of a *King Dhava*, who may have reigned about the fourth century B.C.

Nor did we neglect while in Delhi to visit the various Sanscrit schools which led to our making the acquaintance of some very amiable Pandits. One of them in particular, Bankelal by name, was most attentive to us. Having inherited a large collection of manuscripts from his deceased father, an Indian scholar of some repute, he invited us to go and see them one morning, Mrs. Deussen being also invited to make the acquaintance of his wife on this occasion. The introduction did not take place however, for after he had fetched and led us to his narrow and angular, though by no means unpleasing dwelling, and I proposed that he should keep his promise and take my wife to see his, he begged us to be kind enough to excuse her on the pretext that "lajjate", she was too shy. We turned our attention to the library: it consisted of a kind of press in the wall, in which lay a comprehensive collection of manuscripts, which, judging by the catalogue he produced, must have been in part very old, and perhaps valuable. Each of them was carefully wrapped up in an old green cloth rag, the better to protect it against the ravages of insects, and the unswathing of each of the costly treasures from their modest wrappings proved a lengthy matter. My proposal that he should sell part of them he negatived politely but firmly. On the other hand he made me a present of several manuscripts, amongst others a very old one of the first book of the *Amarakosa.* On our leaving Delhi Bankelâl did not fail to put in an appearance at the station. He presented my wife with a daintily worked purse, the work and gift of his wife, and on our getting into our compartment he took from a servant who walked behind him several trays on which a Hindu dinner was set out, and pushed them into the carriage after us. The dinner consisted of all sorts of vegetables, daintily arranged in little leaf-cups, a great bowl of rice and milk, a pile of chupattees, and a great quantity of sweet dishes, as well as a variety of pastry.

Once more the train bore us away, and once more the curtain fell upon the pregnant picture of a place that left us memories both great and important, enlivened by the acquaintance of friends whom a few days had endeared to us, but from whom we had all too soon to part, in most cases alas! for ever. However, with fresh courage we were travelling on in the most splendid sunshine—it was the 20th December—through an Indian landscape adorned with all the voluptuous charms of summer, and were looking forward to traversing the sacred territory between the Yamunâ and the Ganges on our way to one of the very holiest towns, *Madhurâ*, the theme of so many legends, the birthplace of *Krishna*, a town which we may justly term the Indian Bethlehem. About noon we came to a small and nearly deserted station. The Dak Bungalow being too far off, the friendly station-master assured us that he would arrange for our accommodation either in the waiting-room or in a railway carriage, and we went on in the same train to save time a station farther, to *Vrindaban*, an hour's distance to the north of Madhurâ. Together with *Mahâban*, which lies about the same distance to the south of Madhurâ, Vrindaban and Madhurâ were the scenes of the childhood and youth of the God Krishna. Krishna, originally a human hero in Indian legend, already appears in the Mahâbhâratam as the incarnation of the god Vishnu. In the character of Arjuna's charioteer, while the two armies are drawn up facing each other in battle array, he favours Arjuna in all haste with a philosophical didactic poem in no fewer than eighteen cantos, to inspire him with courage for the encounter. This is the famous Bhagavat-Gîtâ, which teaches that all temporal birth and decay, life and death, are as nothing in comparison with eternity. A farther development of the Krishna story is found in the Purânas, the story of his youth in particular being told in the Bhâgavata Purânam, in a manner most strikingly reminding us of the story of Christ's early years. The seer *Nârada* prophesies to King *Kamsa* of *Madhurâ* that Vasudeva and Devakî shall bring forth a child that shall rise up and slay him. He thereupon causes the parents to be kept prisoners in a house that is shown to this day. Krishna is born there, but the keepers are overcome by a miraculous sleep, the parents flee with the child across the Yamunâ to Mahâban, the King commands that all male children that give promise of heroic strength to be killed, Krishna escapes him, spends the rest of his youth in Vrindaban, till he grows up and slays King Kamsa. The resemblance between the late Indian legend and the New Testament story can be no mere coincidence, and we must perforce assume some Christian influence to have occurred between the period of the heroic epic and that of the Purânas. This assumption is all the more confirmed when on visiting the house of Krishna's birth you are confronted by three clumsy dolls on a kind of dais, representing the child Krishna (the middle figure), with the father Vasudeva and the mother Devakî on either side. It entirely corresponds to the fashion prevalent in Roman Catholic countries of representing Mary and Joseph with the Child Christ.

Putting off our visit to Madhura till the following

day, and leaving our luggage behind with the servant, we went straight on to Vrindaban, the place in which Krishna is said to have spent his youth, and to have played his naughty pranks on the shepherdesses, hanging their clothes high upon a tree while they were bathing for instance, only to be prevailed upon to restore them after manifold and earnest entreaties. Many pictures of this scene are to be met with throughout India. It thoroughly corresponds to the native mixture of religion and sport everywhere met with in India, to find this mischievous Krishna worshipped as a god in many of the magnificent temples. Having got to Vrindaban (properly Vrindâvanam, forest of the Vrindâ, *i.e.*, Râdhâ) we sent the letters of introduction we carried to two Pandits, and meantime wended our way towards the town, but were induced to stop not far from the station to look at a temple which a rich Indian was having erected in the most gorgeous of fashions. We inspected the marble staircases and halls and the costly ornaments, consisting of precious stones, being accompanied by a Brahman youth in a sky-blue garment, who had joined us. With our habitual good-nature we gave him a seat in our carriage, but were afterwards much surprised to have him ask us for money on bidding us farewell; what we gave appearing to be too little in his opinion he actually emphasised the service he had done us, which we had not demanded, nor indeed had he shown us, for immediately after leaving the temple our two Pandits, Râdhâsarana and Madhusûdana, had turned up and undertaken to show us the town. Three or four temples in a good state of preservation were first visited. The gable of one of these was adorned with a perfect host of statues; Krishna performing his heroic deeds or playing the flute for Râdhâ, his mistress, to dance to, was everywhere the most conspicuous figure. A further ornament of the temples and houses, if I may dignify them by such a qualification, were the numbers of living monkeys that played all sorts of antics, climbing up the walls and perching on ramparts and roofs. We met with no such lively monkey population in any other town but Vrindaban, except in Ayodhya, the holy city of Râma; in Benares the amusing animals, having proved disturbing amid the busier traffic, have been banished and relegated to one solitary temple, Durgakund, which to the no small annoyance of the natives the English insist upon calling the Monkey Temple. In Vrindaban a shoal of beggars proved infinitely more troublesome than these harmless denizens of the roofs. It was easy to see that we were in a spot to which many strangers bent their pilgrimage. Though the company of our two Pandits afforded us some slight protection we were almost as incessantly stopped on our way by beggars as in Granada or Jerusalem, many of the fellows being both hale and hearty in the prime of life. I was repeatedly forced to make use of such expressions, "I give to the old, the sick and the destitute, but to you I will give nothing!" These words, spoken in the most dignified Sanscrit, met with full approbation from our Pandits, nor did they fail to make an impression on the curious crowd that looked on. I need scarcely point to the fact that in the smaller places in India a couple of white-skinned Europeans excite just as much wonder as a negro and negress do with us at home when they pass along a street. After having exhausted the sights of the place we were treated by our Pandit friends very much as curiosities ourselves, and conducted by them to their homes, as well as to the abodes of some famous holy men. We did our best to cut the proceedings short, for night was falling and the hour for our train to leave was at hand. At last we managed to get ourselves seated with our Pandit friends on a bench at the station, there to await the train in the refreshing coolness of the evening air. One of the Pandits had a plate of exceedingly doubtful looking fruit brought for our refreshment. I ended by choosing a banana, as presenting the least danger; it proved to be perfectly unripe, resembling a raw potato both in substance and taste; I could not bring myself to swallow the bite I had taken, and had to disappear round a corner to get rid of it and the rest of my banana. I only mention this to show how badly off and how unpretending these Pandits must be. The train being behind time, I had a longer discussion with the younger Pandit, Madhusudana, who was studying philosophy, and was of course a follower of the Vedânta, though of the realistic tendency of the Madhva. His ideas, in consequence, like his character, were somewhat sober, but on the other hand so clear and precise as is rarely met with among Hindus. I cannot put him down as a type of the ideal · enthusiastic Hindu, too prone alas! to lose himself in vague ideas, but I should not hesitate to give him the preference in all things relating to practical every-day life.

Our train now came steaming in; we got into the first-class carriage, easily distinguishable by its white colour, and which proved to be quite empty, though in the twilight we did not observe that everything in it was filled with a thick coating of dust, and in ten minutes we had reached Madhurâ. Here the railway officials had spread the news of our arrival, and we were in consequence received by a deputation, who with genuine Indian naivete informed me that the entire Arya Samâj had assembled in the town, that a carriage was in waiting to take me there; and the hope was entertained that I would give an address as I had done in Agra. "But, dear friends," I replied, "it is 8 P. M., we have touched nothing since noon and we are both tired with our journey. The cook whom you see yonder with his white apron is urging us to have supper; wait at least till I have partaken of something in all haste. I will then come with you to address the meeting in a few words of greeting at least." This proposal met with approval: in flying haste we swallowed our dinner and were then driven off in *Sresht Lakshman Das'* exceedingly elegant carriage to the meeting.

It was nine o'clock by the time we got there. I greeted those present, praised their interest, and, will

I, nill I, had perforce to promise to give the desired address the following afternoon at 5 o'clock. Having bid a brief good-bye we were driven back to the station in the carriage, which was placed at our disposal for the whole of the following day, and dead tired dropped into the beds that had been improvised for us in the waiting room. Next morning when we were on the point of sitting down to breakfast we were told that a fresh deputation desired to wait upon us. They came, they said, from the Dharma Samaj, the members of which in this town were more numerous and more influential. I was therefore requested to give the lecture I had promised the Arya Samâj in the Dharma Samâj instead. "Your Association," I answered, "may very well be the more highly considered in this town, and had I known that earlier, it might have influenced my decision, but at present I cannot entertain the thought of breaking the promise given to the other Association." Would I then, they suggested, give a second address in the Dharma Samâj? "I have not the faintest intention," I replied, "of giving two addresses in one town, the more so as I am travelling for pleasure in India. If you want to hear me come to the Arya Samâj at 5 o'clock this afternoon; you shall all be made welcome."

Thereupon they took leave of us and we started off to see the town in the company of the Pandit, *Bala Krishna*, to whom we had had a letter of introduction, and of some others who joined us later on. On our way I asked the Pandit about his studies.

He was a medical man, *i.e.*, he had studied the Ayurveda, and had an extensive practice in the neighbourhood. "What is fever?" I asked him. "Fever," he replied, "is a false mixture of three of the juices of the body, wind, mucous, and bile." "And how do you cure it?" Here he glibly rattled off a terrific list of drugs, which after having been pounded and mixed were to be administered to the patient.

In the course of this conversation we had reached the Ghattas, the chief sight of the town. They consist of a beautifully paved esplanade-walk, from which numerous well-built flights of steps lead down to the river, and which extends along the river bank as far as the town extends. Stairs and steps everywhere led down to the water and to the bathers, pretty pavilions invited the passer-by to a cosy seat, the river bank was studded with buildings rich in storied lore, an imposing tower for instance being shown us on the spot where *Kamsa's* wife performed her *Sati*, after Krishna had slain her husband. *Sati*, originally signifying "the good wife," *i.e.*, the wife who had herself burnt alive with her spouse's corpse, has a second signification, the *act* of the widow's being burned, and as a third signification the place where such a burning has taken place, and which is marked with a monument. A little farther on we were shown the spot on which *Prabhunârâyana*, the present Mahârâja of Benares, of whom I shall have more to say later on, had himself weighed on the occasion of his visit to Madhura, making a present of his full weight in gold to the Brahmans. This little pleasantry cost him over 1,00,000 rupees, as we afterwards heard in Benares. This munificence inspired Professor Gangâdhara, whose excellent lectures on the Indian poets I afterwards attended in Benares with the greatest pleasure, to write a poem, with a copy of which he presented me. On the title page a pair of scales is painted, in the rods and divisions of which the names Prabhunârâyana, Madhurâ, &c., are divided into syllables and worked into a poem on the following page, a poem so complicated in the verse employed that the author himself saw the necessity for adding a learned commentary.

Our friends took us further outside the town, past wells, the stone walls of which were most brilliantly painted with fearfully gorgeous pictures relating to the Krishna legend, then through a grove to an eminence on which stood the house in which Krishna was born, of which we have already spoken. It was a hall open on one side, in the centre of which on a stone platform stood the three gaudily painted dolls, reminding us forcibly, as we said before, of the figures of the Child Christ with Mary and Joseph, so often to be met with in Southern Europe. Meantime all sorts of folks had gathered round us, each anxious to contribute his mite to our instruction. The most striking figure was that of a beggar, a strong young man, with a handsome body that was almost stark naked, his long shaggy hair standing out wildly from his head, his whole body horribly smeared with ashes. This is the garb of the ascetic, and is copied nowadays by many of the beggars for the sake of the effect it makes on the public. On turning away I gave the oldest of those present a rupee with instructions to divide it justly, but it was my luck to have some of them come after me to complain that they had been overlooked at the division. There was nothing for it but to go back, demand to have my rupee returned, have it changed in the neighbourhood and then dole out a few annas to each according to his merit and respectability. This act of justice was loudly applauded. We then returned to our carriage, and, in accordance with the arrangement made, drove to the house of its owner, a rich *Vaisya*, called *Sresht Lakshman Dâs*, who had got together a meeting of Pandits in our honour. We were hung with chains of gold paper this time instead of with the customary wreaths of flowers, and these chains we still have, while the splendid wreaths and bouquets presented to us elsewhere we had perforce to leave behind.

The afternoon was devoted to an excursion to Mahâban. The way lay across the Yamunâ, an iron railway bridge being open to carriages, though only on payment of a toll of two rupees, which struck us as exorbitantly high. Here I saw a huge shell, such as the ancient Indians used for a war-trumpet, and which appeared to be used on the bridge for signalling purposes. There was a hole bored at the point of it for blowing into; I could not get a sound out of it, and expressed the wish to hear the shell blown. An old woman was requisitioned. who put the shell to her mouth, producing several piercing, shrill tones, surprisingly loud, and carrying to a great distance. At last we drove across the Yamunâ bridge, and then through the pleasant landscape to Mahâban, where in various houses we were shown all sorts of souvenirs of Krishna's childhood. Here again the prejudicial influence of the foreign visitors on the character of the people made itself felt once more; the people proved greedy and discontented with what was given them. After a short inspection of the place, which offers little of interest, we turned our backs on it, got into our carriage again, and punctually reached the hall of the Arya Samaj at five o'clock. The lights were lit, the hall kept filling rapidly, I had the big folding-doors which opened on to a noisy street closed, and began my lecture on the Vedanta. After having given it in English I was asked, as I have mentioned before, to recapitulate the chief points in Sanscrit, many present being ignorant of English. I did so, and now a discussion ensued, half in English, half in Sanscrit, revealing Theistic tendencies to a great extent. I closed the meeting amid the warm applause of my audience, and was accompanied by a great number of those who had been present to the station, where, tired out, we soon lay down on the beds that had been made up on the straw-bottomed benches, and slept as well as it was possible, amid the noise of the trains that passed during the night. Huge swarms of pilgrims spent the night outside the station, squatting

Indian fashion in groups upon the ground. Our servant Lalu told us next morning that he had met acquaintances from his native village, and they asked him if he had neglected to bathe in the Yamuna for the remission of his sins; he, however, had assured them that he had had no time to do so, nor did he feel his sins particularly weigh upon him. Lalu, it seemed, was something of a free-thinker, but he had still worse qualities which were to make themselves apparent that very day. It had happened more than once already that he had overslept himself on our arrival at a station, and I had had to drag him out of his third class compartment. I had also occasionally noticed a peculiar odour about him, but on my asking, "You don't drink, Lalu, do you ?," he always answered most emphatically, "No, Sir."

We got into the train that in the course of a day's journey was to take us out of the Yamuna valley into the Valley of the Ganges, as far as *Fatehgarh*, where we intended to spend the night, our arrival having previously been notified to the railway clerk by letter. Towards evening we arrived, and after some calling and waiting Lalu at last put in an appearance to see to the luggage. He proved to be quite incapable of rolling up and strapping the plaids, and on looking at him more closely I saw that he was perfectly tipsy. "Lalu," I said, "You are drunk." "Yes, Sir," he replied, "Why shall I not tell the truth? I sometimes have a touch of fever, and then I take a drink to fight it down." I made no reply, but his fate was sealed.

With the help of the clerk we got the luggage into the waiting-room, where we were again to pass the night, leaving Lalu to sleep off his liquor in some corner or other with prodigious snorings. We spent the evening in agreeable converse with the clerk, a man of considerable mental parts. He did his best too, to get us another servant, but in so small a place it was not possible to find someone suitable at such short notice. So we had to put up with Lalu for the next day at least. He put in a shame-faced and seedy appearance the following morning; I studiously avoided addressing him and took our three tickets for Cawnpore.

On arriving at Cawnpore after a six hours' journey, during which I had vainly attempted to get a sight of the Ganges, which flows hard by, we were at once welcomed at the station in German. It was Herr Bassler, a capital young merchant, whose acquaintance we had made on board ship, and whom we had promised to go and see in Cawnpore, where he lived. We had accordingly sent him word of our coming, and there he was at the station with his little carriage, insisting on taking us to spend the night in his bungalow. Bachelor though he was, we should want for nothing. We accepted his kind invitation, and I only asked him to wait at the station until I had settled accounts with Lalu. I sent for the sinner and mildly but seriously admonished him for his fault, informing him that I had to dismiss him. He tried what prayers and promises would do, but there was no getting over me. I paid him the wages due to him, as well as his ticket back to Bombay, with something over and above, and the long row of silver coins seemed to reconcile him to his fate. I shook hands with him kindly, adding a few admonitions for the future, and he disappeared, to be seen no more.

My wife got into Herr Bassler's light tamtam, which he drove himself, and I followed with the luggage in a second carriage. We drove to Bassler's bungalow, taking a glance at the chief sights of the town on our way. They consisted of a Memorial Church, a disused well, surmounted by the beautiful statue of an Angel, and other monuments, all referring to the Mutiny, as the English term the Rebellion of 1857. Had the rebels attained their end, and for a time there was some prospect of their doing so, they would have been held in honour by their nation, as we honour Schill, Scharnhorst, Blucher and the other heroes of the Wars of Independence. As they were overthrown they are now termed mutineers and their memory decried, so prone is mankind to bow down to success, which is all too often a mere matter of accident. After having made a pilgrimage to the bank of the Ganges, our first glimpse of it, here already a mighty and majestic stream, we got to Herr Bassler's bungalow. It furnished us with a welcome picture of how a German bachelor, though exiled to India's shores, can make a cosy home for himself. From the street we drove into a spacious compound, in the middle of which stood the square, one-storied house, comprising several halls with bedrooms on either side. They were simply but comfortably furnished; in our bedroom we found two good beds, and a mirror was even produced later on. In these apartments, Herr Bassler was master of all he surveyed, and lived as a rule quite alone. He had no fear for his own safety, his bedroom being furnished with a little arsenal of weapons, the best-approved and most elegant of their kind. Europeans living in India are furnished with them gratis, the natives on the other hand being almost entirely prevented from owning arms, owing to the heavy import duties and other obstacles laid in their way. In the case of an insurrection a small, but well-armed army of Europeans would at once spring up out of the ground, so to speak.

Herr Bassler of course was surrounded by half a dozen servants, who all lived outside the house in little huts in the vicinity. These servants do not render any very great service, each of them only doing his own particular work, but they cost very little, for they are neither lodged, clothed nor fed, but get five to ten rupees a month, on which they not only live, but keep their families. Some of them deftly served us a very good dinner, being however ordered about rather more than seemed necessary by their master, who was evidently exceedingly strict with them. He declared this to be necessary, else the fellows would become unbearable. After Herr Bassler had said, "Boy, cheroot!", the servants at once brought the desired cigars, which we put in our mouths as we lay reclining on sofas, or with our feet upon chairs, the servants kneeling to give us matches, the work of puffing being all that was left us to do. We sat up a long time chatting cosily. Herr Bassler told us about his home, a little town in Saxony, and how he was living in India as the agent for a firm yonder, managing the purchases of grain and skins. He told us about the crocodiles he was in the habit of shooting in the Ganges, of the dangers of the Indian climate, and how a friend of his had died of cholera one night after having spent the evening quietly playing at cards with him. On the whole I fancy that the tales he told were intended more for travellers less acquainted with the country than we were by this time. Of course the subject of snakes came in for thorough discussion; we heard how fatal the bite is, death following in a few minutes, how the reptiles slip into the houses at night and are even to be found in the beds, so it was with somewhat heated imaginations that we betook ourselves to rest. In the middle of the night I woke, and heard something rustling in a corner; I listened; it came nearer, and circled round my bed snuffing and spitting. I did not dare to strike a light lest I should irritate my gruesome visitor by the movement; I anxiously listened to the noise, and heaved sigh of relief when it at last withdrew, and silence once more reigned. Herr Bassler to whom I told my story next morning thought it must have been a musk-rat; these rats are frequently found in the houses, but are perfectly harmless.

Next morning when we were returning with Herr Bassler from a walk in the adjacent gardens the new servant Herr Bassler had got hold of for us put in an appearance. His name was Purân, *i. e.*, the Old One, and really was about sixty, and in consequence rather lazy and somewhat of a slow coach, but with plenty of experience and self-assurance. His English too was much better than Lalu's broken attempts at the language. In religion he was a Mahomedan, though one of his certificates described him as a Christian. My wife unhesitatingly gave it as her opinion that the man was likely to suit us and was quite ready to engage him. I was all the more glad to hear this, as servants seldom succeed in satisfying her, and, as it turned out, her complaints of Purân later on were both frequent and bitter. Purân was accordingly engaged, we partook of a hasty breakfast at Herr Bassler's and then took the train as far as Lucknow, a short journey. Neither the summer-like weather nor the behaviour of the people we met reminded us of the fact that it was Christmas Eve; for there was nothing Christmas-like in the appearance of a band of Scotchmen in fantastic disguises, who played comic songs in front of the hotel after dinner. I retired to the drawingroom, where Mr. Summers joined me, and I played him some German Christmas carols on the piano. He was about to start for Allahabad next morning to attend the National Congress, and there, as I have already mentioned, he died of small-pox a few days later.

In Lucknow we found ourselves much in the same situation as a man in the habit of wearing spectacles, who has mislaid or lost his eyeglasses. Everything in consequence looks indistinct, cloudy, less beautiful. The spectacles we stood in need of in Lucknow were the friendly natives who had usually been at hand to act as guides elsewhere. Our Bombay friends, it is true, had taken care to give us a letter of introduction to an excellent man in Lucknow, Madhura Prasâd, but unluckily he happened to be away from home for two days, and did not call upon us in our hotel till the evening before we left (December 26th). He was accompanied by his son, a boy of ten, with whom I had a little talk in Hindustani, in which I had so recently begun to take an interest. Hitherto I had only heard it spoken by coachmen and servants, and it was a perfect pleasure to me to hear the purity with which the child expressed himself in his native tongue.

We spent the afternoon after our arrival in wandering about the streets of the big city pretty much at random, for we could not manage to procure a plan of the town; Constable's excellent Hand-Atlas of India not having yet been published at that time (1895). Next morning we decided to go about things more systematically and to begin by doing the Residency which lies pretty much in the heart of town. It consists of a complex collection of half-ruined buildings and fortifications, which are carefully preserved in this state, being the memorable spot where from July to September 1857, a thousand English people, men, women and children, were besieged by the rebel sepoys, exposed to the most terrible dangers and privations.

all the time. Every detail of this memorable episode was vividly recalled at sight of the half-ruined buildings, and their immediate surroundings. We saw the vault in which the women and children had crowded together, to seek protection from the rain of bullets, the room in which Sir Henry Lawrence, struck by a splinter from a grenade, breathed his last. Opposite was the House of John, from which an African inflicted tremendous losses on the besieged, and a little farther off was the cemetery, with its monuments, and the graves of about two thousand persons who fell victims to this catastrophe.

On our way back from these sad scenes, after a long stroll through the town, which is spaciously built, and well supplied with gardens and squares, I noticed a big wooden building a little way back from the street; posters announced that Sakuntalâ by Kâlidâsa was to be performed that evening by a Parsee Company. I decided to go to this performance. After dinner my wife, who was tired, retired to our bedroom, which, as is customary in India, opened straight on to the verandah. There being neither lock nor bolt, no infrequent occurrence in India, there was nothing for it but to barricade the door as best I could with the assistance of the servant, and then set off with him for the theatre. The temple of the Muses was about half an hour's walk from our hotel. Vainly the servant shouted and whistled for a carriage; there was none to be had. At last we managed to get hold of an ekka, the most miserable vehicle that it has ever been my fortune to drive in. We both sat down on the floor of the cart, our legs dangling, and off our sorry hack trotted into the pitchy darkness of an Indian night. There was a lantern, it is true, but it did nothing but keep going out; if kept open the wind blew out the flame, if shut the flame died out for want of air. At last, however, we got to our destination, and told the coachman to wait for us till the performance was over. Spreading a blanket over his steed, he squatted down at its forefeet, as Indian coachmen are wont to do, and promptly went to sleep. We got out and I was respectfully conducted to my seat in the front benches, which were very empty, though the back benches were well filled. My servant was allowed to enter free of charge. The public was entirely native, I being the sole and single European who had happened to stray in. The play began, it was Sakuntalâ, but alas! Sakuntalâ in the guise of an opera. It was in all probability the same performance my friend Garbe had seen in Bombay, and of which he speaks so contemptuously. I must acknowledge him to be right; the thing was not only long, but dull. Sleep all but overmanned me, and I had to have recourse to a cup of tea to refresh myself. This was served in the open air in the pauses. Finding that by one o'clock we not got beyond the first act, I considered I had had enough of it and started for home accompanied by Punân. Our coachman was still quietly seated at his horse's feet, sound asleep. After we had roused him he set up a tremendous wailing and lamenting, for someone had stolen his horse-blanket, the only thing in the cart worth stealing no doubt. We comforted him with the gift of a few coins and had ourselves jolted home.

The following days we spent partly in seeing the Mahomedan edifices, in which Lucknow abounds, partly in going to see several manufacturers of clay figures, types of Indian national costumes, and trades. Lucknow produces very fine specimens, though the prices cannot be called cheap—10s.—and more were asked for a well-finished figure about ten inches high.

The Hindu friend to whom we had been recommended did not appear in our hotel till the evening before we left Lucknow. He spent a few pleasant hours with us and provided us with an introduction for *Fyzabad*, the station for Ayodhya, the city of Rama, the next goal of our pilgrimage.

Early in the morning we took the short journey from Lucknow to *Fyzabad*, and, having secured rooms in the hotel, made our way to the house of the man to whom we bore introductions. Unfortunately, he too was away from home in consequence of the holidays, so after a pretty lengthy conversation with a friend of his who happened to be at his house and who gave us a certain amount of information about our intended destination, we decided to set out for Ayodhya by ourselves. No time was lost in procuring a carriage, our servant jumped up beside the driver, and we bowled along to the famous city of Rama. With the exception of a few gigantic broken columns here and there,

there was nothing to remind us that we were traversing the scenes of so much past glory. In less than an hour we had reached *Oudh*, built on the site of the ancient Ayodhyâ. It lies on the shores of the majestic *Sarayu*, and like *Madhurâ*, its numbers of temples stamp it as a holy city, not to speak of its hosts of monkeys disporting themselves on all the roofs and squares, and painfully but respectfully kept at arm's length by the vendors of eatables. Some grains of corn had been scattered on an open space under some trees, and a rush of monkeys ensued, who crushed the grains in their paws, closely scrutinising them before swallowing them. Down the road came a few sheep, led by a boisterous ram; he butted aside the apes most unceremoniously with his horned head, and set himself to finish up the grain. The monkeys' efforts to put the intruders to flight by making the most atrocious faces at them were unavailing; they had at last to content themselves with the scanty grains they could manage to pick up without running any risk, making funny little dashes at them between the hind legs of the sheep. We left this little scene to enter a neighbouring temple, to which many people were crowding; priests stood on the steps in front of it, who took vessels containing milk and fruit from the people and after pouring a portion of the contents into larger vessels, returned what was left to those who had brought them. I could find nobody who could give me any information respecting this strange custom.

We now climbed up a hill on which stood a Mahomedan temple, consisting as usual in India of an open hall. Our servant, having obtained leave to bathe in this holy spot, absented himself for a quarter of an hour, and we were left to ward off as best we could a number of indiscreetly inquisitive persons—Mahomedans. We descended the other side of the hill, passing through tobacco plantations, said good-day in passing to an old scholar who was engrossed in the study of the Sânkhya philosophy, and strolled back to the town along the beautiful river-bank. We came past a large temple to Râma. I wanted to enter and was somewhat brusquely refused admission. In vain I explained in Sanscrit that I had studied the Râmâyanam, and that though a foreigner I was far more worthy than many another to pay my homage to the hero Râma. My explanations served no purpose, perhaps they did not understand me—at last I got angry, gave vent to a short sermon of remonstrances, and turned my back upon the inhospitable portal with the words "*kruddhosmi!*" (I bear you a grudge.)

The tropical sun was low in the horizon when we got into our carriage and bade farewell to the site of the ancient city of Râma. Ten minutes' drive took us to a hill on which Buddha is said to have preached. We climbed it, and on the top found a half-ruined house with a pretty little garden. A friendly old couple were the guardians of the spot, and with them we exchanged a few words, while enjoying the extensive view of the city and the plain with its river gleaming like silver in the rays of the setting sun. Then we went back to our carriage and drove on to *Fyzabad*. At dusk we reached our hotel. At dinner there was one other guest besides ourselves, a painter, who showed us a fine collection of Indian landscapes. "Here," I remarked, "we have a painting with clouds, reminding us of our landscapes at home." To which he made reply, "You must not say that; these clouds are entirely different to those of our northern sky."

Next morning saw us at the station again. We took tickets for Benares, where we arrived at the very hottest hour of the day, after a three hours' journey. We took up our quarters in Clark's Family Hotel, having at first a room on the ground-floor to the left; as soon as there was more room we got a ground-floor room on the right, in which we spent three weeks. The hotel is close to the street. On the opposite side of the street there was a church in spacious grounds with beautiful gravel walks and flower-beds. Shady shrubs grew there too. With the help of stones fetched from a ruined well, it was quite easy to get over the low wall separating the churchyard from the road, so we availed ourselves of this opportunity every day and enjoyed strolling about the churchyard either by ourselves or with the visitors who came to see us, and whose conversation occasionally threatened to become too loud when several of them appeared together and the debate became lively, no matter for surprise with such naive children of Nature as the Indians are. When sitting in the hotel verandah with a group of professors or pandits in native dress, it was easy to read in the faces of those who came and went that our presence was none too welcome, so we got into the habit of establishing ourselves on chairs in the shade of the churchyard bushes on the other side of the road, where tongues could wag without let or hindrance.

Beyond the church lay large open lawns. Professor *Venis*' house lay there, a little farther came his father-in-law *Lazarus*' printing-press and bookshop; then came the post office, and at last the outlying parts of the town, which must have been at least a quarter of an hour distant. The town itself, extending in a semi-circle along the left bank of the Ganges, is a perfect labyrinth of narrow, winding streets and alleys, which the stranger finds some difficulty in threading without a guide, the more so as at that time there was no detailed map of the town in existence. We had to make our way through this maze of streets every time we wanted to get to the Ganges, which is the chief sight of Benares. The banks are both high and steep here, and along these heights are ranged the palaces of foreign princes. and various club-houses. Numbers of staircases, the so-called Ghattas, lead down from this row of buildings to the Ganges. Every morning, summer and winter, the same amusing spectacle can be witnessed on these river-staircases. The shore presents a lively scene of groups of bathers every morning at seven o'clock, a daily bath in the Ganges being prescribed by the Hindu religion, as well as being a most welcome diversion. By going to the *Dasâsvamedha Ghatta* early in the morning, and hiring one of the big high boats, of which there are always plenty, you can have yourself rowed down stream, and have ample opportunity of getting a close view of the groups of the men; at a little distance from them the women can be observed in clusters, splashing about merrily in the water, while engaged in washing clothing and utensils. Their thin garments are spread out to dry on the stones on the shore, and by the time the owner has had his bath and left the water, the intensely hot rays of the morning sun have sufficiently dried the clothes to make them fit for wearing again. On going farther along the shore you come to a spot, where from early morn to dewy eve the corpses of those people are burned who have come to live in Benares on having attained a ripe old age, in order to die there, or the corpses of people who, before dying, have specially willed that their remains be transported to Benares. As several funeral pyres are generally burning at the same time, it is quite possible to get an idea of the whole process in a very short time. The corpse wrapped in sheets and wreathed in flowers is first carried in by bearers, and the first thing done is to push it and the plank on which it lies half way into the river, and from there, after the pyre has been built, it is taken and placed on the big wooden logs, of which the pyre consists. Other logs are placed upon the corpse, and the pyre is then lighted by members of a certain privileged caste, in whose hands the whole ceremony lies. The flames blaze up, spreading from log to log, and at last seize the corpse; the relatives of the deceased stand at a little distance meanwhile, watching the proceedings in apathetic silence. In a few hours the corpse is entirely consumed, all but a few fragments of bones, which are then cast out into the Ganges. The lazy current is covered long after with charred fragments, wreaths, &c. Meantime a new pyre has already been erected on the place that has just become vacant, in preparation for the next forthcoming corpse. There are nearly always quite a number of pyres burning at the same time, and the number of corpses burned in Benares is very great, the Indians believing that the burning of the corpse in Benares enables the soul at once to enter into salvation. Lower down the banks are less busy; by following the river for about half an hour you come to the spot where the *Varanâ*, a streamlet about twelve yards broad, flows into the Ganges, forming the limit of the town on the one side, while the almost dried-up bed of the *Asî* upstream forms the opposite limit. These two rivers have given the town its name—*Vâranási*, *i.e.*, Benares

On an eminence on the opposite bank, higher up the stream, lies *Râmanagaram*, the residence of the Mahârâja of Benares. It consists of a spacious palace and offices, with an adjacent temple to Durgâ.

We had had our letters of introduction to the Mahârâja presented at once on our arrival in Benares, with a request for an audience. The following day the

Mahârâja's Secretary appeared in the hotel, and our visit was arranged for the following day, December 31st. At the hour fixed the Mahârâja's carriage fetched us from the hotel, and in it we drove to the Ganges. A litter with bearers was in waiting to transport my wife down the bank to the river, a royal craft took us across the river, and in litters we then proceeded to the palace. The Mahârâja received us with a large retinue, consisting chiefly of Pandits. The political power having passed almost entirely into the hands of the English, most of the Indian Mahârâjas are little more than rich and highly honoured gentlemen of private fortune. Many of them are addicted to luxury and sink into debauchery, others make use of their influence to further religion and science. This was the case with the present Mahârâja of Benares, Prabhunârâyana, who had succeeded to his father only a few years before. Though he was already the father of a grown-up son, who afterwards made his appearance, the Mahârâja made the impression of a youngish man, gentle and modest in bearing. He spoke very tolerable English, as well as Sanscrit. The conversation was conducted chiefly in Sanscrit, out of consideration for the Pandits present, who took an active part in it. From time to time the Maharaja had a costly pipe brought, which he returned to his servant after taking a few whiffs at it. The request I proffered of having some Pandits sent to me every day to practise Sanscrit conversation was most readily complied with. The Mahârâja besides placed a handsome carriage, coachman, and two footmen, at our disposal for the whole period of our stay in Benares. It may give an idea of this man's riches and piety, to mention that in Madhurâ, a sacred spot, he had himself weighed, and then had his weight in gold, some 100,000 rupees, I was assured, presented to the Brahmans. We have already mentioned this fact, as well as the Sanscrit poem in which Professor Gângâdhara extolled the incident.

After a conversation of some length in a magnificent hall, the Mahârâja offered to have the palace shown to us, and we paid a proper tribute of admiration to the costly ivory carvings and other works of art. The Sakuntalâ room proved most interesting; in it there were pictures illustrating the chief scenes in the Sakuntalâ drama. Much gratified we said good-bye, carrying with us the scent of attar of roses, with which our hands had been sprinkled from a precious vase when we bade farewell.

A few days after the Mahârâja returned our visit, a palace not far from the hotel being chosen for the occasion. The number of Pandits present on this occasion was still greater. We spoke of Germany, and I had some difficulty in making them understand in Sanscrit the description I gave of our northern climate with its ice and snow; most of the Indians have never seen snow, hence the difficulty in giving them an idea of it. Suddenly the Mahârâja rose up to go, inviting me to accompany him in his carriage, my wife following a few minutes later on in another carriage with some of the ministers. The conversation during the drive which was partly in English, partly in Sanscrit, was chiefly about the journeys the Mahârâja undertook to his dominions in the south, journeys frequently taken on elephants. In answer to my question whether he did not think of coming to Europe one day, he replied with a decided negative. On my remarking that the Mahârâja of Baroda happened to be in Europe at the time, he answered very shortly, "Oh, he is a Sudra." We drove to see *Bhâskarânanda Swâmin*, a famous saint, to whom the Mahârâja desired to introduce me himself. As it turned out I had already happened to make his acquaintance. The young Pandit, Venirâm, with whom I had had Sanscrit conversation lessons in Bombay, had told me that his father was leading the life of an ascetic in *Asîsanga* near Benares, and had given me a Sanscrit letter to him. Soon after our arrival in Benares we had made our way to Asisanga, where after repeated inquiries we were at last directed to a garden in which a naked hermit lived. His sole clothing consisted of a small loin-cloth. He took the letter, threw a careless glance at it and gave us a most kindly reception. He was not Venirâm's father, however, and I never got an opportunity of making the latter's acquaintance. The hermit was Bhâskarânanda Swâmin, and it was to him that the Mahârâja now conducted me. This time he was stark naked. The way in which this poor ascetic, who could call nothing in the world his own, received the rich and noble Mahârâja, made a great impression on me. He received the Mahârâja, who approached with a bow of great humility, with condescending familiarity, and greeted me, welcoming me as an old acquaintance and fellow-student of the Vedânta, without further ceremony. He bade us both sit down on a stone slab, seated himself beside us so cleverly as partially to conceal his want of clothing, and began a most animated discussion on the Upanishads with me, I all the while in the embarrassing dilemma of knowing my wife might arrive at any moment and find him in his garb of primeval simplicity. I repeatedly mentioned that my wife was expected immediately, but he paid no heed to these remarks, and not until my wife and her companions were seen approaching through the trees, did he ask for a rag, which he considered ample preparation for such a visit. The Mahârâja now took leave of us, while Bhâskarânanda had the proofs brought of an edition of the Upanishads at which he was working, and which has since appeared. This furnished us with ample food for conversation. Later on he sent for a fruit, which he peeled and prepared, insisting on putting pieces of it into my wife's mouth, as well as into mine, with his own brown fingers. When he said good-bye he made us a present of a mango-fruit, which a pilgrim had brought him from the far south, where everything ripens earlier than in northern India. Though this saint kept his vow of absolute destitution, to which he no doubt owed in great part the veneration with which he was universally regarded, though there was nothing on earth he could call his own, yet he cannot be said to have wanted the common necessaries of life. His vow prescribing stark nakedness, and this being forbidden in the town by a police regulation, he passed his days in a fine big garden. placed at his disposal by one who venerated him. Here he wandered about in the shade of the trees, writing his works, and receiving the visits of the faithful. Many of them were in the regular habit of sending him food, others looked upon it as a kind of special favour to be allowed to serve him. When I went to see him another time in the company of my wife and Mr. and Mrs. aus dem Winkel, a young couple from Dresden, he showed us everything there was to see in the garden, addressed the two ladies as "Mother," and was most touching in his endeavours to be of assistance to them in going down the steps of the stone staircase, though the discomfort was far greater for him with his bare feet and limbs than for us. I asked him where he slept. He showed us a little stable-like shed, the floor of which was covered with straw. Here he slept without any further bed or bedding, both summer and winter. He next conducted us to another shed, situated lower down, in which a sculptor was at work carving a colossal marble statue of our saint for one of his admirers. The sculptor had tried his "prentice hand" on a couple of miniature statuettes in stone. I bought one of them, a very good portrait of Bhâskarânanda's face and figure, and I am still proud to call this quaint curiosity my own.

I had been impatiently waiting for January 4th, 1893, to arrive, the day on which the University lectures were to begin again after the Christmas vacation. Henceforth I regularly attended the lectures at the Sanscrit College of the University every morning from 7 to 9 o'clock. The Sanscrit College is a department of the University, in which the various sciences are taught for the natives in the ancient fashion, and according to the classic Sanscrit text-books. The language used was always Sanscrit, at least in all the lectures I attended. I much enjoyed Professor Gangâdhara's lectures on grammar and literature, Professor Sudhâkara's on astronomy, Professor Râmamisra's on philosophy, as well as a number of others. The lecture-rooms in the University are large and lofty, surrounded by open halls and gardens. All doors are left open during the hours of instruction. Two or three professors often teach in the same room, each occupying a corner with his little group of pupils. We are accustomed to see a row of hats hanging at the entrance to the lecture-rooms; in India you are confronted instead by a collection of shoes, for both professors and students do not remove their turbans during the lecture, but take off their shoes. They find it strange that the European, on entering a room, which is cooler than the outside world, should remove his head gear, which they regard as an ornament, while retaining his dusty shoes. It would be impossible too to keep on one's shoes without dirtying both the floor of the apartment and one's own clothes in the cross-legged attitude they affect. Chairs, tables, and benches are conspicuous by their absence; professors and students sit cross-legged upon the floor. Any writing that may have to be done is done on the palm of the hand, and a rest for the hand, if offered, is refused, as inconvenient. Punctuality cannot be said to be one of their chief virtues. Many come after the lecture has already begun, others leave before the end, entering noiselessly and squatting at the feet of the master, to retire as quietly. There were seldom more than six grouped about the master. The master pronounces the word "*alam*"=enough, at the close of the lecture, though sometimes the pupils forestall him, with the cry of "alam."

The University, or rather the College of Benares bears an English character, but the Sanscrit College, though it forms part of it, is most pronouncedly Indian in all appertaining to it. The various sciences, grammar, law, philosophy, even astronomy and medicine, are here taught in accordance with the ancient native hand-books. The absolute dependence upon Indian antiquity, the solution of every dispute by a reference to the ancient authorities, as well as the discussions of their axioms, remind one strongly of mediæval teaching in Europe; equally mediæval is the strict adherence to all sorts of superstitions, which both limit and dominate the ideas of learned and intellectual men, in a most extraordinary manner. The earth, for instance, stands still, the sun and stars revolving round our world; the serpents found infesting the ancient walls of dwelling-houses are looked upon as the souls of their forefathers; death in Benares is followed by an immediate entry into salvation; these and other similar superstitious fancies are met with even among the most learned of Pandits. Much, however, as the works of Indian scholars stand in need of rectification at the hands of European science, as little can a European ever attain that marvellous command of Sanscrit which with Indian scholars is a mere matter of course. They speak Sanscrit as fluently as if they had never spoken anything else, and they read the texts they interpret so rapidly that it is difficult to follow even with the eye. In a two hours' lecture Gangâdhara expounded a whole act of the drama *Mâlatimâdhavam*; on my asking whether there were texts he was unable to read at first sight, he answered that that very rarely occurred. The astronomer *Sudhâkara* developed the most difficult mathematical-astronomical problems in fluent Sanscrit with the help of the most primitive instruments and *Râmamisra* interpreted the *Sânkhya-kârikâ*, as well as the commentary to the *Vâsaspatımisra*, with scarcely a glance at the book; he seemed to know not only the Kârikâ, but the whole of the compendious commentary by heart. "Sanscrit," he said to me, "is as familiar to me as my mother-tongue." In striking contrast to the fluency of his Sanscrit was his clumsy English, which he was at no small pains to display in our conversations, so that I had frequently to insist upon his having recourse to Sanscrit. His philosophy was based upon the Sânkhyam, to which the Vedânta has degenerated, not upon the pure doctrine of the older Upanishads and Sankara's revival of them. A debating meeting was arranged for the discussion of these questions, but I need scarcely say that I did not succeed in converting him from his realistic views, which were rooted in and founded on the Râmânuja. On my way home from the meeting, one of the students present joined me, and told me that he was far more inclined to my conception than to his master Râmamisra's. One Sunday afternoon I was sitting with Râmamisra among the rose-bushes in the churchyard opposite the hotel, deep in philosophical talk on the nature of the soul. He looked upon it as an immaterial substance inhabiting the body, somewhat in Descartes' way of thinking. I had just cornered him with the dilemma that either his soul possessed *pratighata* (power of repulsion), and was then unable to penetrate the skull and other material obstacles, or did not possess *pratighata*, in which case it was unable to move the limbs of the body, or wander from one place to another, when a well-dressed young Indian joined us, following our conversation with deep interest. His name was *Govind Dâs*, and he owned an elegant house near Durgakund, above the town. Like all well-to-do Hindus he had a carriage and horses of his own, and often came to take us for drives. He did not speak Sanscrit, but good English, and used to dub himself "a busy idler," *i. e.*, a man who profited by his material independence to devote himsilf to literature.

Govind Dâs took us to his house, which lay in the middle of a fine garden. In one of the rooms a number of wedding presents were displayed, gifts to a newly married member of the family. To our astonishment, in place of the statues, clocks, lamps and show-pieces we are in the habit of presenting, we saw an array of sacks, containing various kinds of grain, trays of fruit and similar gifts of provisions, some of which had no doubt a symbolic meaning. He then took us into his library; the walls were covered with books, almost the whole of the room being filled up by a big table which in India is used, not for sitting at, but sitting on. It is only a foot higher than the floor, and is covered with grey linen. The student sits cross-legged in the middle of the table, the length and breadth of which permits of his surrounding himself on all sides with piles of books. In summer, we sometimes sit at work in our shirt-sleeves, the Indian scholar takes his ease by dropping his upper garment as far as his girdle and sitting naked as far as the waist. Interesting as I found all this I was very little edified by the contents of the library. The Vedanta was represented, but in its latest and most corrupt form, and then came a great collection of modern theosophical works, for our friend Govind Dâs was an enthusiastic theosophist. With the deepest reverence he laid before me a number of ponderous and most elegantly bound volumes, containing the wildly imaginative flights of Madame Blavatski. It is a source of regret to observe how the noble philosophic instinct of the Indians is being led aside into false paths by theosophism, which is now so rife in India. Colonel Olcott of Calcutta is at present at the head of this movement. I did not see him in Calcutta, but accidentally met him later on. When returning from Calcutta to Bombay we had a ten minutes' stop at Moghal Sarai, a railway station opposite Benares on the south bank of the Ganges. I got out on to the platform and was taking a last farewell look at Benares, with all its pleasant memories, when Govind Dâs suddenly came up to me, and at once offered to make me acquainted with Colonel Olcott who happened to be there. We bowed, each conscious of having long known of the other and his opinions, and aware that nothing could ever reconcile ideas so opposite as ours were. My train starting precluded any further conversation, and cut short our reserved but by no means unfriendly interview.

I should like, however, to say something of the other interesting impressions we got of Benares during our stay of twenty days. Raghunandana Prasâd completed our learned circle of acquaintance. He was a barrister at the Benares Law-Courts, and at the same time a member of the Municipal Council, in which capacity he had access everywhere, and the way in which he took us about Benares was both interesting and instructive. Early one morning we took a boat with him, and had ourselves rowed past the merry groups of bathers of both sexes. We passed through a labyrinth of narrow lanes to get to a holy place, called the Inânakûpa or "Well of

Knowledge," a by no means inviting spot, almost rivalling Egypt in the impertinent begging that went on there. The Hindus too cannot be got to refrain from throwing flowers and other gifts into this deep well, and in consequence these things decay, and pollute the air. Our friend showed us measures he had taken to intercept the things thrown in order in some measure to prevent this nuisance. Our way now led to the two large minarets which tower above Benares as landmarks. They were erected by the Mohammedan conquerors, as a symbol of their domination over the most sacred town in India, to the great annoyance of the Indians, until they learned to bow to the inevitable, and introduced the two minarets into their own religious system, explaining them to be two Krishna pillars. One of the minarets is at present closed, owing to its ruined condition. We went up a winding staircase in the other and from the top had a magnificent view of Benares, lying in a half circle on the Ganges, and of the surrounding country, studded with houses and gardens. Our intelligent friend now took us through the poorer quarters of the town. We saw the weavers at their work, weaving the most beautiful fabrics at the most primitive of looms. We saw the potter, as he cowered on the ground, setting his huge wheel in motion, throwing a formless mass of clay upon the centre of it, and producing a dainty vessel in a few seconds. We took one of them, which had just been baked hard at the fire close by, as a keepsake, and so far it has escaped breakage. Our road led on through narrow streets, past numerous temples, Benares being said to boast five thousand, though many of them do not exceed a dog-kennel in size. Towards evening we witnessed a wedding; the ceremony was over and the entertainment, which was to last all night, had begun. The entertainment consisted in the male guests, about a hundred in number, seating themselves in a great hall on the floor, and watching with rapt attention the performances of the dancing-girls, hired for the occasion. The girls stepped forward, one at a time, dressed in gold-embroidered garments reaching to their feet. They sang monotonous love-songs, accompanying them with equally monotonous movements of their arms and bodies. The most they can be said to have done is that they kept turning like teetotums, it cannot be called dancing. One being tired, her place was at once taken by her fellow, who proceeded to go through the same evolutions. We felt decidedly bored by the whole business, and the bridegroom, a lad of fifteen, seemed much of our opinion, for, though seated in the place of honour in the middle of the company, he was fast asleep. Towards eleven o'clock we took our leave, and on our way home had an opportunity of observing in what holes and corners of the streets the homeless were trying to get a night's rest.

We cannot say good-bye to Benares without referring to the intercourse we had with some of the younger Pandits. I had asked the Mahârâja to send me one or the other Pandit for the practice of Sanscrit conversation; and from that day there were three who took turns in presenting themelves every day in our hotel, to spend the greater part of the afternoon with us. They were the pious and gentle-minded Priyanâtha, his brother, the sturdy, clear-minded and steady Pramathanâtha, and the younger and more lively Bahuvallabha. The only way of communicating with them was by talking Sanscrit. My wife generally managed to make herself understood by signs and a little Hindustani, so we were able to gain an insight into the hearts and minds of these men. Priyanâtha, our most regular visitor, was a faithful, reverent soul, the author of a few articles on Sânkhyam, &c., and just in him I had occasion to note that the Indian sense of religion has exactly the same effect upon their spiritual life as Christianity upon ours. He set aside my suggestion that he should go to England, with the remark that his faith forbade that, and on my pointing out that, after passing the higher examinations in England, he could attain a better position in his own country, he quietly answered that eternal welfare was far more important than things temporal. He too believed that dying in Benares entailed immediate entrance into the state of salvation. I reminded him that, according to the Scriptures, he only attains salvation who possesses knowledge, no matter where he happens to die, but not he who is ignorant of knowledge, even though he die in Benares. He informed me thereupon that, by a special favour of Siva, perfect knowledge was conferred upon all those who died in Benares when they breathed their last. Occasionally.

we spoke of the political situation of the country, and I was struck with the deep and hopeless grief the intellectual and sensitive Indians feel at seeing their country ruled over by a race differing so widely from them as the English do.

A particular proof of Priyanâtha's confidence was his consenting to take my wife and myself to his house and to introduce us to his family, with the very natural reservation that my wife only was to be admitted into the presence of the ladies of the family. She managed to carry on a limited conversation in Hindustani with them. The Pandit lived on the upper floor of one of those large houses built round a central court, the various stories being provided with wooden verandahs. The furniture was of the simplest; the various pieces of furniture reminding us of those we had seen in Luther's room in the Wartburg; in fact, it altogether made a very mediæval impression. It was the last evening of our stay in Benares, so we determined to have a row on the Ganges, and got into a boat belonging to the Pandits or to their master, the Mahârâja. From the fields on the opposite bank we got a full view of the sacred city, with its twin minarets, its flights of steps down to the Ganges and its numerous palaces and temples.

On Tuesday, January 17th, 1893, we drove to the station, accompanied by the three Pandits, and in a last conversation with them I had a renewed opportunity of admiring the elasticity of Sanscrit, which makes it possible to express oneself with ease on all the achievements of modern culture, such as the railroad, the engines, and so on.

In a few hours the train took us to Bankipore, an important railway junction, situated on the Ganges, close to Patna, the ancient Pâtaliputra. We had an introduction to Mahesa Nârâyana, the Editor of the Behar *Times*, a weekly paper. After a long search we found him and he placed himself at our disposal in the most obliging manner, giving us much valuable information concerning the town and its surroundings. At my request he conducted us along a clay road to the shores of the Ganges, which rolled its yellow waters between slopes which were covered with cornfields. We gazed in amazement at the traces of the devastation the river yearly causes, when it changes its bed, entailing a fresh distribution of the soil. Towards evening Mahesa Nârâyana had to bid us good-bye. What we then undertook and where we found quarters for the night have, strange to say, entirely escaped my memory, which is the more astonishing as every other detail of our Indian trip is clearly present to my mind even after a lapse of ten years. My attention may have been diverted by the excitement with which I was looking forward to the following day. Next morning we took tickets on a narrow gauge line, and after travelling three hours to the south, reached Gaya, the holy site of Buddhism. The line lay through hollows, past forests of palms, beneath the crowns of whose young five-yard stems pots were fastened, to catch the plam-juice oozing from the cuts made above them. This is the Tâlî, or toddy as it is now called, which we were to become acquainted with in Calcutta. We noticed numbers of beggars behind the railings at the various little stations we passed. I cannot get the picture of one man out of my head who, clothed in an apron, had crept up to the railing on his crippled limbs, and kept scratching his emaciated arms between the bars. He was perhaps the most miserable specimen of humanity I had ever seen. He reminded me of the apparitions, the sight of which made Buddha, the prince's son, become a homeless beggar.

Gaya is a little country town, and, allowing for the differences attendant upon its Indian site, may be said to bear the characteristics typical of so many small towns in Germany and the rest of Europe. There is no hotel, but as elsewhere where a hotel is wanting, a Dak Bungalow or Rest House, kept up by the Government. In it every traveller may lay claim to one night's quarters at least, at the rate of one rupee per bed. There is generally a cook on the premises who, according to tariff, provides tiffin for 1½ rupees, and dinner with two meat courses for two rupees. We ordered dinner for the evening, took possession of a room, and soon after got into the most miserable of country carts, to have ourselves jolted along a fine broad road, through wooded fields, to Buddha-Gaya, a distance of about one hour and a half. The place consists of a cluster of houses by the wayside; to the left of the road lies a monastery of Brahman

Sâdhus, while to the right lies a great temple of Buddha in a hollow, care having been taken to prevent the debris of ages raising the level of the soil. This is surely the spot where the sublime one sat under a fig tree in that great night in which he received his Buddhahood, for Buddha lived long enough to point out the exact spot to his numerous disciples. In the interior of the temple, on the spot where he sat, there is now a gilded giant statue of Buddha, Farther-Indian in type, and to-day as then he sits under a fig tree, though separated from it by the temple wall, a descendant perhaps of the original stock. Steps lead to the next story, with a verandah running round it, and from it a fine view is obtained of the numerous scattered monuments round about, erected by the Buddhists of various countries to the perfect one, in this for them, holiest spot of the world. The place is inspired with weighty memories, but in Buddha-Gaya, as everywhere else in India, there was not a single Buddhist to be found, with whom we might have exchanged impressions. Our examination made, we sought a vain substitute for a Buddhist in the monastery of Brahman monks. We sent in our names, and were introduced into a spacious court, in which the monks were carrying on a busy trade in corn and oil. A staircase led to a big graded terrace lying high where the prior solemnly welcomed us at the head of his monks, some thirty in number. The whole party seated themselves in a half-circle round us, the prior being in the middle, with a young man at his feet whose presence was as it proved of the highest importance, for he was the only one of the whole party who could carry on a conversation in Sanscrit. The prior, to whom of course I addressed my remarks, listened, nodded, smiled, ejaculated a word here and there, but the task of answering fell to the youth at his feet. The latter showed us over the monastery after the audience was ended. We then crossed a field and in the distance could see the chain of hills, at the foot of which Rajagriha lies. The stony clay soil we were walking on seemed to point to the neighbourhood of a river-bed, and I asked our guide if he could take us to the brook Nairanjanâ, so frequently mentioned in Buddhistic writings; the young man at once replied "You are in the very middle of it." The Nairanjanâ, like so many other little Indian river-beds, had completely dried up, though it was only the month of January.

The approach of evening warned us that it was time to start back. We bade the sacred soil of Buddha-Gaya farewell, got into our wretched vehicle and set off for Gaya. The drive was so insufferably slow and jolting that I preferred to walk back in the cool of the evening, going on ahead for some distance and then waiting till the carriage with my wife had made up on me. Though somewhat anxious about meeting with snakes on the road, I enjoyed the Indian evening as I walked through the wooded country; the sun had ceased to dart its glowing beams, and a gentle zephyr filled the air with fragrance.

Our Gaya impressions were less harmonious. The coachman, though amply remunerated, proved dissatisfied and kept abusing us for a considerable time on the big square in front of our rest-house. Dinner was ready. The two regulation meat courses consisted of one chicken, first one half being served and then other, both halves tolerably tough, the creature having evidently been freshly killed.

Next morning I employed the time till our train left in going to see a pretty large temple lying above the town. Being alone I was received with suspicion, the conversations I tried to enter into halted, and on my stopping in front of a niche I was asked to go away, being informed that a Srâddham (sacrifice for the dead) was being performed, and that the presence of a stranger was prohibited.

In the afternoon we got back to Bankipore again, but unfortunately we did not meet our friend of the day before, as he had been called away unexpectedly on business. We took our tickets for Calcutta, and towards evening got into the night express. The first-class carriages were all very full, and we were already resigning ourselves to the idea of a broken night's rest, when I heard that our train was due in Calcutta at 5 A. M. by the direct line, but that another train, after passing one of the first stations, travelled along a loop line, making a detour to the north, and arriving at Calcutta about 10 A. M. To change our minds was the affair of a moment. We got out of the one train and into the other, in which we had a first-class compartment to ourselves and consequently a good night's rest. Next morning we found ourselves at Chandranagaram, which, with Pondicherry, is all that is left to the French of their Indian possessions, and which mere vanity induces them to retain, for there can be little if any profit to be had from this narrow wedge. Here we saw the first Bengal Pandits, tall fine-looking figures, with a profusion of black hair, and a garment, the front point of which descends like an apron as far as the feet. Despite the fierceness of the sun's rays they never wear anything on their heads. They display a certain vanity, not only in dress, but in speech and bearing, and it is not a mistake to characterise the Bengalis as the Frenchmen of India.

CHAPTER VI.

CALCUTTA AND THE HIMALAYAS.

IT WAS nearly eleven o'clock when our train ran into the Calcutta station. It lies on the other side of the Hugli, a broad arm of the Ganges, across which a long swing-bridge leads to the town. It had just started, but we did not find time hang heavy while we waited. We could watch the groups of men and women bathers near us, while along the other bank of the river a number of so-called ascetics had their camp. We have already spoken of these individuals, in reality little more than beggars, who practice a cheap asceticism to impress the people. Each has a pet speciality of his own; one keeps holding his arms in the air, another stands on one leg, with the other drawn up and tightly fastened, a third lies on a bed of wooden nails. Each and all are surrounded by a group of spectators, much as idlers with us congregate about a tinker at his work; a copper is thrown to them from time to time, and this appears to be the end and object of their doings.

It was twelve by the time we at last got across the bridge and had found quarters with some difficulty in Mrs. Monk's Boarding-house. Board costs seven rupees a day, slightly more than in the Great Eastern Hotel, but it is said to be better in quality. The cooking really was very good, but the company the most uncongenial we ever met with in India. Serious conversation was entirely out of the question, cricket, croquet, shooting, and tennis being the sole topics discussed, if we except the never-failing abuse of the natives, to which all young Englishmen are addicted, a result perhaps of the tropical climate. For curiosity's sake I shall chronicle a discussion of this kind. The question was mooted whether an English club ought to accept a challenge to a match if the challengers were a native club. Some negatived the question on the ground that the natives were too inferior to English people to permit of such competition. The other party supported the principle that every challenge, even a native one, ought to be accepted, for, as the speaker characteristically said, "Even should the London chimney-sweepers' club challenge us, we ought not to refuse the challenge." The manners, as well as the conversation, of these young merchants were exceedingly curious. As long as the ladies were present their behaviour was irreproachable. When the ladies left us after dinner the whole company sprang to their feet and remained standing until the last lady had left the hall, until even the last "spring-chicken," who had stopped to say a word in passing, had vanished. As soon as the ladies were gone however, young England made up for the enforced restraint. The young men lounged in all sorts of positions, short pipes were produced, and one of my neighbours, tilting back his chair, went so far as to put his feet on the table at which we had just been dining. For that matter we neither looked for nor found any intercourse with the diners, our whole day being amply filled with impressions of a very different kind.

There was the town itself, the biggest in India, which in contrast to the many others we had seen was not Indian, but more than half European in character. Everything in it, the disposition of the streets, the very names, the squares, and innumerable other matters reminded us of London, the inhabitants too being far more impregnated with and varnished over with European culture than those elsewhere in India. This was particularly striking in what regarded religion. In Western India it is the Aryasamaj that prevails, as we had occasion to mention in speaking of Lahore, here it is the Brahmasamaj, a religious community based like the former upon antiquity, but which, in contrast to the purely national Aryasamaj, has adopted a number of Biblical ideas, as well as some of the Christian rites. Our friends took us to one of their services one evening. It was held in a big building, reminding us somewhat of a Christian Church, with its pulpit and galleries. Printed leaflets were distributed and the contents sung. They were verses from the Rig-Veda, but just those, the hymns to Varuna, in particular, wearing some resemblance to the penitential psalms of the Bible. We had then a regular sermon on a Vedic text, so the European influence was marked. The same may be said of the family life. Our best friends, P. L. Roy, a barrister, and P. K. Roy, professor of Philosophy at the Sanscrit College, with their families, led quite European lives. They wear European dress, sit on chairs at meals, eat meat, drink wine, and are exceedingly tolerant in their ideas. Our amiable friend, Mrs. Roy, was a Brahman of the Brahmasamaj sect. Her unmarried sister, Miss Chakravarti, having been educated at a Boarding School in England, had been metamorphosed into a Protestant, and a third sister, whom I did not get to know personally, had got entangled in the nets of the Roman Catholic *padres* in Calcutta, and to the great sorrow of the family, had become the bride of Heaven, and gone into a Convent. She had, I may observe, a very large fortune. In spite of the diversity in religious opinions, the most perfect harmony reigned in the family, not even disturbed by the visits of a young Mohammedan gentleman who occasionally dropped in as a friend of the family, a strong contrast with his rough boisterous manners to the gentle, sensitive, and intellectual Mr. Roy. His manners may have been a result of his religious faith which stamps not only the individual, but by the law of heredity, whole races as well.

As tolerant as P. L. Roy's family in religious questions was our second friend with his wife and children – P. K. Roy, Professor of Philosophy at the Sanscrit College. He invited us to dinner, and after the meal was over, we retired to his study, unheeding the remonstrances of the ladies, and had a long talk about Plato, Kant and Schopenhauer, with whom he was well-acquainted, and about whom he had many questions to put. For later in the afternoon he had arranged a meeting of about twenty Pandits in our honour, among whom there were several of the most eminent professors at the Calcutta Sanscrit College. I was an attentive auditor at their lectures in the days that followed. I have retained the best possible recollections of three of them, though their names have escaped my memory; the principal, a portly gentleman of refined bearing, who lectured on logic after an ancient Sanscrit text-book; a younger professor, who lectured on the Kâthaka-Upanishads with great gravity and fervour; the third was an elderly professor of literature, whom they all treated with the greatest reverence, and whose beautifully-shaped forehead reminded me of Kant's. He was not only a scholar remarkable for his eminent parts, but distinguished as being the author of several dramas. He interpreted the Kâdambarî, and I have a lively recollection of his having begun to read a perfectly interminable sentence, and remarking as he turned over the leaves "To get to the end of this sentence I must skip twelve pages." As had been the case in Benares, Sanscrit was the only language spoken during the hour's lecture, but there was no sitting on the ground here, the five or six students—I never saw that number exceeded—sitting on chairs round a table, where there was ample room for them all.

Besides the P. L. Roys and the P. K. Roys, we were very friendly with two brothers Mullik, shipbuilders with a yard on the other side of the river Hughli. We went to see the yard one day, and I was astonished to find the numerous workmen shaping and hammering the glowing bars of iron just as our own workmen do, except for their being almost starknaked, which must expose them to frequent burns from the spattering of the hot iron. They were engaged in repairing a big freight-vessel, which had gone on fire at sea with all her cargo. All the iron girders of the hull had been more or less bent. It was both troublesome and costly to repair all this and restore things to their primitive condition, whereas it would have cost incomparably less to have the vessel made sea-worthy regardless of appearances. The ship, however, had been insured, and the owner could demand of the Insurance Company that the vessel be repaired and restored to its original state, so he had no interest whatever in curtailing expenses. The Mullik brothers lived with their mother in a palatial residence in town; they often took us there in their elegant carriage, or took my wife for a drive if I happened to be engaged. They frequently invited us to dine with them, both in European and in Indian fashion. The Indian dinner differed in no way from a luxurious English dinner, except in a few trifling changes, due to the climate. We sat on chairs, ate meat and drank wine, as we do at home. Indian evening-dress consists of trousers and an elegant shirt, shirt and trousers being kept together by a *cummerbund* or silk sash; no waistcoat is worn, and the picturesque attire is completed by a wide short jacket.

12

Those who do not happen to possess such a jacket are either forced to perspire fearfully in a European evening coat, or to appear in walking-suit of thin linen or silk. Most people in India, the English excepted, are exceedinglly indulgent in questions concerning the toilette. Professor Peterson used to cross the street after sundown on his way to a party bareheaded, and there must be many who follow his example.

A native dinner, to which one of the Mulliks invited us was highly original. First of all we were separated, my wife dining upstairs with the ladies off silver plate; I got my dinner downstairs, Mr. Mullik keeping me company, but touching nothing himself under the pretext that it was his fast day. It is nothing unusual for an Indian dinner to consist of twenty courses, half of which are sweet dishes, composed of the most multifarious preparations of milk, butter, rice, vegetables, potatoes, farinaceous foods, and fruits; only meat, fish and eggs being excluded. This time, however, Mr. Mullik wanted to show me what a vegetarian kitchen can achieve, and no fewer than eighty dishes were served, all of which my amiable host was at the trouble to explain to me in detail, while I contented myself with merely tasting the dishes presented. Strangely enough there was one dish of meat among the eighty, most appetisingly cooked too. About half an hour's distance from Calcutta lies a temple to Kalighatta, and Mr. Mullik happened to be one of its patrons. Every morning at 10 A. M. a goat is sacrificed to the goddess Kali, its head being firmly held in a kind of iron fork and struck from the trunk with one single cut of the sword. The flesh of the goat may be eaten, and is looked upon as particularly conducive to health, but is of course very rarely obtainable. I partook of it with a certain reverence, and I am thankful to say was none the worse for it, nor for the rest of the tremendous repast set before me.

Another dear friend was Hara Prasada, a man of frank, lively character with a sound education. He had formerly been a professor of Sanscrit, but had given up this post to occupy the more lucrative and influential one of Councillor in the Administration of the Province of Bengal. As such it was his allotted duty to report to the Government on all the literature printed and published in Bengal. I had quite a number of discussions with him on the Sankhya system, but even he did not succeed in making this most involved of all philosophical system perfectly clear to me. Years later after having completed my studies of the Upanishads I have got to understand the Sankhya system and its epic antecedents, and have proved it to be a realistic transformation of the idealism of the oldest Upanishads. In the second part of the first volume of my history of Philosphy I have traced the gradually progressing degeneration of this original idealsm through its various stages of pantheism, kosmogonism, theism, down to the atheism of the Sankhyam..

Hara Prasada lived with his family in idyllic retirement at the village of Naihati, half an our by rail from Calcutta. There are still a number of Brahman schools, or rather boarding-schools, there. In the old traditional way a number of scholars live in the hut of a Guru (teacher), for whom they do the housework, even beg for him if need be, and in return are instructed in the Veda and other doctrines. Hara Prasada took us with him to Naihati one day, introduced us to the teachers, showed us their houses, and arranged a meeting of about sixty disciples for us. I had to take the lead at this meeting and put all sorts of questions to the scholars, in Sanscrit of course, and they answered in the same language, some of them exceedingly well too. The usual ovations were shown me at the close of the meeting, and incredible as it may sound Hara Prasada, in the presence of the assembled teachers and disciples, hung over my shoulders the sacred sacrificial cord (*yajnopavitam*). This would have been almost on the verge of profanation, had they not been careful to remove one of the strands composing the sacrificial cord beforehand. After the meeting had broken up Hara Prasada showed us the beautiful environs of Naihati, took us to his own house and introduced his son to us, a lively boy of eight, whose great beauty was all the more evident as he came running up to his father in the street absolutely destitute of clothing, addressing me politely with "Good morning, Sir." His father told me that the boy had already begun to learn the most important Sanscrit words from the Amarakosa;

this quite explains how Indians attain a fluency in Sanscrit which Europeans can never rival.

I owe many other impressions to the ever-obliging Hara Prasada, who was never at a loss when applied to. For instance, I had expressed the desire to see a Kokila close at hand, which is by no means easy, as these Indian Cuckoos are exceedingly shy. Indian poets extol the beauty of its song, as we do the nightingale's. He excels the latter in the clearness and force of voice, but his song is less varied, for I never heard more than two motives any time I happened to hear him. The one motive consists in an incessant repetition of keynote and fourth, the other in his occasionally running up the scale from key-note to octave chromatically. I had never managed to see a Kokila, and my delight was great when Hara Prasada one day entered our apartment, followed by a servant carrying a cage with a Kokila in one hand, a huge pot of freshly-tapped toddy in the other. We admired the Kokila, which though as black as a raven, was not unlike a pigeon, yet more slender and more delicate in shape. We then partook of the toddy, which as long as it is fresh tastes not unlike rather weak lemonade, and is a perfectly harmless and favourite beverage among Indians. If kept, it ferments in the course of a few hours and becomes exceedingly intoxicating, strong in taste and like a liqueur. We decided to try the experiment, and had four little bottles filled and hermetically sealed at a neighbouring chemist's. We put them into our trunk to make the voyage to Europe. Thereupon, we started upon a four days' trip to the Himalayas, and on our return found that the perfidious beverage, in fermenting, had exploded the corks and made its way through all the packing papers, with dire results to the things it had been packed with. There was nothing for it but to throw away the all but empty bottles, and content ourselves with the odour the palm-wine had conferred on books and other of our belongings.

The above mentioned four days' trip to the Himalayas is one of the most interesting episodes of our Indian sojourn, and I am far from regretting the twenty-four hours' railway journey from Calcutta to Darjeeling, for the mere chance of gazing upon a Himalayan landscape, and then setting off back again. It may be compared to a North German setting out for Interlaken, merely to enjoy the sight of the Jungfrau for a few hours, and then starting off straight home again. Most people travel up from the fiery furnace of Bengal to Darjeeling, some 7,000 feet higher, to spend a few months there, and restore their health in the magnificently bracing mountain air. The temperature there is never lower than 42°, and never more than 60°. The English are worldly wise enough to issue no return tickets on this line being no doubt sure that those who travel up are forced, will they, nill they, to travel down the same way, without any reduction in the fare, there being no other way of getting down.

Having sent on our luggage to Mr. Roy's safe keeping, as he had invited us to stay with them on our return, we made our way to Sealdah Station on February 1st, 1893. We had given our servant a four days' leave of absence, and started alone for the North at 3 o'clock in the afternoon. At 8 o'clock we had reached the Ganges, across which at this point there is no bridge, owing to the extreme breadth of the river. The passengers were taken across in a steamer, a good supper being served on deck. On reaching the opposite bank we made haste to take possession of an empty compartment in the train awaiting us, and were lucky enough to secure one to ourselves.

While we were having an excellent night's rest the train kept steaming northwards all night. On looking out of the window after dawn we were delighted to get our first view of the lofty blue Himalaya range. Unlike the Alps, which are so pleasingly broken in their groups, the Himalayas rise solemnly and majestically in one unbroken line. In Silguri, the railway proper comes to an end, and while breakfasting we had plenty of time to admire the prettiest of little toy-railways, which was to take us up to Darjiling in eight hours. The principle adopted in building this railway had been to avoid all tunnels and to get to the top by a series of almost innumerable windings. Very occasionally a very steep slope necessitates the train having to climb the mountain-side in a succession of sharp zigzags. Owing to the numerous curves it has been found imperative to lay the rails as close together as possible, in fact, they are only two feet apart, the carriages themselves being but four feet broad. To ensure safety in travelling upon so narrow a gauge, the point of gravity has had to be laid as low as possible, and, in consequence, the floor of the carriage is scarcely a foot higher than the ground. The wheels run inside the carriages, but so covered as to avoid all danger. Most of the first-class carriages are roofed, but open on all sides else; they have two front and two back seats. We got into one of these carriages, having taken due care to wrap up well, for the temperature on the heights is exceedingly cold. The sturdy little locomotive that was to drag us up, puffed and panted away, speeding first for over an hour across the plain, which is coverd with tea plantations, and then began the region of the Terai—as the lowest slopes of the mountains are termed—in which the water often collects in great swamps. With their fever-laden air they are as dangerous for man as they are beneficial to the vegetable kingdom. Giant trees and clambering creepers grow here in wild and luxuriant confusion, baffling the eye that would attempt to find its way through and over the abundant vegetation. High above the tallest trees huge ferns rise, completing a picture that no man can imagine who has not gazed upon it, and the picture once gazed on, can never be forgot. It takes about an hour to get through this unhealthy region, then the train, like a serpent spouting fire, begins to mount higher and higher in innumerable winding curves. On looking back, the Plain of Bengal keeps receding farther and farther; the panorama varies every moment; one is fain to seize on every new phase, and loath to let it pass. The lower spurs of the mountains, which from below looked like massy, towering mountains themselves, now lie far below us in the abyss; we can look down upon their highest peaks from where we now are. Yet, the slopes of the Himalayas are far less rugged than those of the Alps. The train crawls along the ledge of a precipice far less seldom here; I can only remember one such spot, to which the English have given the name of Sensational Point. The train works its way up higher and higher, clinging to the right wall of a huge mountain gorge, and avoiding all the overhanging promontories by a series of innumerable curves. Here and there from amid the forest the miserable huts of a mountain hamlet peep forth; a few of the inhabitants stand at the stations begging for alms. Their Mongolian type, with its yellow complexion, broad face, flat nose and prominent cheek-bones, forms a striking contrast to the Indian of the plains. We inhale the pure bracing mountain air with delight, though we begin to feel it decidedly cold. About noon we reach Korscheong Bazaar, the lunch station, where we have a halt of twenty minutes, and then on again in three hours as far as Goom, the highest point on the railway. On the walls quite close there was real snow at the beginning of February, the only snow we saw all that winter. An ugly old woman went begging from carriage to carriage, gesticulating grotesquely. Everyone who has been to Darjiling will remember her a the witch of Goom. Shivering a little, we take our seats again. The railway descends a little, makes a detour round a knot of mountains, and at four o'clock steams into the station of Darjiling, the terminus. Here there are only three kinds of roads, straight up, straight down, or a winding path on the same level. No carriages were to be seen. A few women took possession of our luggage to carry it to Woodland's Hotel, and we clambered after them. We asked for rooms. The Manager drew a long face and asked how long we meant to stay. I was quite prepared for being turned away when I said that we should only be able to stay two days, but contrary to my expectations the man's face brightened and he said, "Then you can have the best rooms. The entrance is from the big terrace, and you get a full view of the mountains from the terrace, or the rooms. even from your beds. through the glass doors and windows. The day after to-morrow I must have the rooms however. for the whole suite has been reserved for the Austrian Prince and his party." The mention of the Austrian Prince made me smile, for we had heard of him already in Calcutta, of his ignorance of Sanscrit and of Hindustani, his English even being so limited as to necessitate his having recourse to an interpreter. But that did not prevent his travelling to India! We took possession, had a good fire lighted, a novelty for us that winter, and turned our attention to the second biggest mountain in the world. We saw nothing however but a dense wall of fog, though more adjacent mountains and the picturesquely situated Darjiling were quite distinct. At our feet lay the station where the sturdy little locomotive was just panting his last puff for the day, deeper down was the market-place, where the mountaineers of Sikkim, Bhutan, and Nepal barter their wares; on and on the path went, down and ever deeper down, past the Botanic Gardens and the Tea Plantations, till it was lost in the endless abyss below. But what was all to us if we were to be deprived of our sight of the snow mountains? We were comforted with the assurance that the view generally cleared for about an hour at six a. m. We spent the rest of the day at home, hoping that one or the other of the two Indians to whom we had sent our letters of introduction would come to see us in the hotel. Our messenger, however, brought back the answer that the one was away from home, while the other lived out of Darjiling at some distance and would not come into town to his office till next morning. Someweat disappointed we went to bed betimes, lest we should sleep too long next morning and miss the magnificent landscape nature here offers.

Our first glance on waking was at the snow peaks; contrary to the expectations which the hotel people had held out, they were still wrapped in clouds. We got up and went for a walk, still hoping that during the day the mountain would lift its cloud-cap, if only for a second, a vain hope as every one of any experience could at once have told. Our immediate surroundings had to make up to us for the want of prospect. The weather was splendid; following the paths along the verge of the precipice the eye could plunge into fathomless valleys, in which the wreaths of vapour assumed fantastic shapes as they rose and fell. We went as far as a hill on which a Buddhist shrine was situated. The quantities of tawdry flags with which it was adorned on the outside made it look far more like a booth at a fair than a temple, and the devil masks within had nothing that could impress the soul with a feeling of sanctity. These means suffice to satisfy the metaphysical requirements of these simple mountain folk. For, in contrast to India, where there are no Buddhists left, everyone here is a worshipper of Buddhism, though of a Buddhism that has developed from its originally pure ethic doctrines into a chaos of superstition and fantastic ideas. The people are as modest in the other requirements of life as in those concerning their faith. Their lot is one of laborious toil and scanty earning, and yet they are as cheerful as the sparrows. Everywhere they are to be seen chatting, singing, laughing, a striking contrast to the earnest melancholy Indians of the plain. Owing to the want of driving roads, stone and all building materials in Darjiling have to be carried up the mountain in creels, a task women are employed in. We saw them climbing up with their burdens, stalwart, buxom figures—we even made the acquaintance of one of their number. As she passed us on the way up with six heavy stones in a creel on her back, a stone fell. She could not bend to pick it up, nor was she able to set down her creel, as she would have been unable to get it on her shoulders again without help. Seeing her embarrassment I gallantly stepped forward and replaced the stone in the creel, for which she thanked me with a look of gratitude. I was thus enabled to get a good look at her, and noticed that she wore not only all her jewelry, but all her "gear" in the shape of a number of copper and silver coins with holes in them, hanging in chains from her neck to her waist.

We spent the forenoon in this way, and on our way back went into the curiosity shop, which is kept by Mr. M. He was visibly pleased to have a chance of talking to countrymen of his own. He showed us all his treasures, such as devils' masks, flags, skulls, arranged as drinking goblets, and Buddhist praying wheels. The written prayers are placed in these, and the wheel turned, each turn being equivalent to a repetition of the prayer. The Buddhists we see are even more practical than the Roman Catholics, who have to keep repeating their prayers while taking part in pilgrimages and processions. Our Lord forbade to use vain repetitions, as the heathen do, and gave us as example a short simple, heart-felt prayer—the Lord's Prayer. What would He say were He to see His Prayer thoughtlessly gabbled over and over by the sheep of His flock? The Buddhism of to-day is merely an enlarged edition of the errors of Catholicism.

Towards noon our Indian friend appeared in the Hotel. He was a big, handsome man with a full black beard and hair curling round his expressive brown face.

Of course, we spent the rest of the day with him. He took us to the market-place, the centre of commerce not only for the Province of Sikkim, in which it lies, but also for the tribes of Bhutan, which lies farther east, and of Nepal on the west. Sikkim and Bhutan are peopled by a Mongolian race of Buddhists, the inhabitants of Nepal, however, are of Indian extraction, and our friend was a native of Nepal. The natives of Nepal are the only people left in India who have hitherto escaped subjection to the English yoke, owing to their mountainous home and their prudence. They do not throw their country open to Europeans in the tolerant fashion that has proved so fatal to the rest of India. Anyone having business in Nepal is conducted with his passport to the capital, Khatmandu, is permitted to see to his affairs, and is then obliged to leave the country. Nepal can boast to owning the highest mountain in the world, Gaurîsankar, which the English have somewhat arrogantly named Mount Everest, after the man who undertook geometrical measurements on it. When one hears English people in India asking each other "Did you see Mount Everest ? &c.," we must pity them for not knowing that this mountain owed its original beautiful and sacred name to Sankara, *i.e.*, Siva, (whom Kâlidâsa already extols as the highest deity, the incarnation of the Atman,) and to Gaurî, his consort. Gaurî and Sânkara's nuptials have been described by Kâlidâsa in the beautiful poem, Kumârasambhava with all the glowing colours of the tropics and the East. And this magnificent twin-peak that bears the name of India's most sacred gods is now profanely dubbed—Mount Everest.

From the Darjiling market-place our Nepalese friend took us downhill to the Botanic Gardens, affording a most interesting insight into the vegetation of the Himalayas. He wanted to take us still farther downhill to a tea-plantation, but a cuttingly sharp wind, bringing with it great dust-clouds, warned us to wend our steps homewards. The whole day long we had not got a glympse of our snow-mountains, though our conversation at the cosy fireside with the noble Hindu did much to atone for our disappointment. This man, like all the better class Indians we had met with, was full of grief at the subordination of his native land, the Nepalese feeling themselves thorough Indians. He confidently hoped for the appearance of a saviour, a kind of Messiah, of whom he spoke with all the fervour of a prophet, who would break the foreign yoke, drive out the Mohammedans, and restore India to all its old power and splendour, which if we examine things more closely never really did exist after all. The Indians were always too noble-minded and intellectual not to be trodden beneath the feet of the brutal superioritty of desire—first, by the Brahmans, and kings of their own race, then by Alexander and his Greeks, by the Bactrians the Skythes, the Arabs, the Mongols and the Europeans. We talked till a late hour, when our friend bade us farewell, a definite one – for as I said to Mrs. Deussen, "We cannot stay on here day after day in the uncertain hope of seeing the mountains one morning. To-morrow at 10 A. M. we start back to Calcutta."

Next morning on waking I was surprised to find everything unusually bright. I sprang out of bed and hastened to the glass-door leading to the verandah. Who can describe my delight on seeing the whole range of Kanchinjinga, the second highest mountain in the world, spread out before our gaze in cloudless splendour, with all its gorges, crags and peaks, up to the two golden horns glittering in the sunshine, the *Kâncana–cringa*, from which the Pandits derive the name. All too certain that the spectacle would not be of long duration I rushed myself to the empty kitchen in search of our boots. We dressed in flying haste and hurried through the deserted streets of the little town to Observatory Hill, to get a still better view of the prospect. On the way we met Mr M., the curiosity-dealer already mentioned, out for a walk with his dog. We invited nim to accompany us, and he led us to the best point to get a view. Here an immensely wide and deep valley stretched itself between us and the mountain, on the other side of which it rose, visible from its base to the incredibly lofty peaks, an immense snow-covered mountain-giant. I was able to distinguish the highest peak in the middle, the two less lofty ones on either side of it, these again being flanked right and left by lower horns. Mr. M. proved most useful, though I must beg leave to make him entirely responsible for the accuracy of what follows. "On the right," he said, "between the two last horns you see a black cut. That is the pass leading to Tibet at a height of 21,000 feet through eternal snow. I myself have mounted to a height of 20,000 feet, but was forced to return, as it is not possible to make such a journey across absolutely desert glacier regions without a great retinue of bearers and guides. From the pass to the highest peak is still 8,000 feet, which you can here take in at one glance. The other, still higher mountain of which you speak, and which as I cannot remember its other name, I must term Mount Everest, cannot be seen from Darjiling. To see the highest mountain of the world you would have to go to Tiger Hill, a good hour's distance from here. I do not however advise you to do so, for from Tiger Hill you would not see more than three tiny peaks, like little sugar loaves, owing to the mountains that lie between. But make haste for the sun is rising higher, and soon the view for to-day will be over." We now witnessed a marvellous spectacle. Misty clouds, which till now had been crouching like sleepy monsters deep down in the valleys, began to set themselves in motion, once roused by the sun's beams. Slowly and lazily they crept their way up the mountain sides, languidly receding from time to time. With ever more success however they rose and began their attack upon the highest giant peaks. Single banks of vapour, tailing away into the weirdest of shapes, now rose to the very highest peak, only to sink again, until at last, reinforced by auxiliary masses from below, their victory was complete. For one moment the three highest peaks gleamed through the veil of mist, only to be at last entirely submerged in the sea of clouds. "Is there any chance of its clearing again?" I asked our companion. "No more hope of that to-day," he answered. We returned to our hotel highly satisfied. The impression was all the more precious, as, chary at first of its favour, the mountain had proved all the more generous in what it had at last deigned to disclose. To those whose fortune it is to stay longer in Darjiling the sight of this prodigious mountain landscape may come to be matter of custom, and elicit no further astonishment, but this was not to be our fate. We did not take leave of the mountain, but the mountain of us, which is properly the finer and better way of it.

At 10 o'clock we bade lovely Darjiling farewell, and our gallant little engine took us downhill at the same pace at which we had mounted, neither slower nor quicker, the journey, however, being a little more exciting, as we we were compelled to look down all the time. At Koerscheong Bazar, where the trains meet, we saw an old acquaintance for a few moments, who was on the way up. It was a Mrs. Davidson, a good old lady from Scotland, who was making a similar tour through India as we were, with this difference that she always made a point of going to see the people we were most anxious to avoid, the missionaries. We had dined at the same table at Watson's Hotel in Bombay, and she had used sometimes to bring a missionary with her to make up the quartette. On one occasion I took the opportunity of telling this reverend gentleman that on visiting the Pinjra Pol (Indian Animal Hospital) I had asked my Indian friends to show me the department in which, as I had been informed, Negroes were specially kept that their heads might furnish happy hunting grounds for vermin. My Indian friends had laughed in my face, and told me that such an institution had never existed, and was an invention of the missionaries. I was curious what our reverend friend would say in answer. He simply repeated that there had been such a department in the Pinjra Pol, that it might even still exist, so to avoid insulting him I dropped the subject. With Mrs. Davidson, our table neighbour in Bombay, we had shaken hands and said *Au Revoir*, without ever dreaming that we should cross each other's paths again. Strangely enough we came across the lady no fewer than three times in the course of our trip through India, though our meetings were of the briefest. Our first meeting was at Koerscheong Bazar, the second at Madura in Southern India, and the third the day before we set sail for home, at the post-office in Colombo.

On reaching Siliguri at the foot of the mountains, we found that we had not such a good connection back to Calcutta as we had had on our journey north. We did not cross the Ganges till after midnight, the mighty current glittering in the magic light of an Indian full moon. Though half asleep I was struck by the curious way in which the railway halls and sheds were built, all of thin laths, and looking as if planted in the soil. On inquiry I learned that the river often changes its bed here, and that, for this reason, the station with all its buildings had to be so constructed as to be easily transported in case of necessity. On we went through the pitch-black Indian night, hailed the rising sun at this, the most easterly point of our wanderings, and got to Dum-Dum, the last station before Calcutta, safe and sound in the early afternoon. Here by appointment we met Mr. Roy and his family, to see the Agricultural Exhibition, which had just been opened. There were horses, oxen, cows and calves, agricultural implements, &c., &c. I took no interest in all this, and was much astonished at the crowds of visitors showing far more interest in these frivolities than in the wonderful tropical surroundings, as well as far more interest in our pale Eurpean faces than in the brown faces and picturesque garb of their own race.

We retuned to Calcutta with the Roys, whose hospitality we had accepted, so that we had now an opportunity of getting an insight into family life in India. Mrs. Roy's sister, the delicate and lovely Miss Cakravartî, (whom the English have re-named Chuckerbutty)—the one who had gone over to Christianity in England, without the slight detriment to the innocent charm of her character—had vacated her room for us, and there we settled down among knick-knacks, photos, and dainty paintings. The family consisted of two children, charming little Hindu girls, who as usual in India were attended upon by a horde of servants. It is quite impossible to keep up a respectable house in India without a dozen servants at least. The highest is the butler, who looks after his master's wardrobe, and waits at table; then there is a ladie's maid for the mistress of the house, and a nurse for the little ones. Frequently, the latter accompanies the family to Europe and Ayahs as they are called, are no uncommon sight in London. Next in the list of servants comes the cook (Bâvarchii), with his assistants; the porter; the coachman; the washerman (every house having its own, for fear of infection,); the gardener (Mali); the water-carier (Bhisti); and last, the lowest in the category the Mehtar or sweeper, as the English call him, whose duty it is to be always at hand to remove all excrements at once. As a rule an Indian house is extremely clean and appetizing, odours being conspicuous by their absence, as the kitchen is not usually in the house itself, but in an adjacent building. These servants get wages varying from five to twenty rupees per month. They get nothing but these extremely low wages, neither food, clothing, nor even accommodation. They live somewhere near at hand with their familes, come only to do the duties required of them, and then return home. The cost of the service in such a house comes to about £7-10-0 a month.

Not only did Mr. Roy entertain us in the most hospitable manner during the rest of our stay in Calcutta, but he was constantly at pains to procure us new and interesting impressions. One of the most interesting was a visit to a very holy penitent nun, who happened to be in Calcutta at the time.

A friend of Mr. Roy's had offered to procure us an

audience at 8 o' clock one morning. A servant fetched my wife and me at an early hour and told us all sorts of marvels about the saint on our way there. She was a Princess from the South, had owned six lakhs (6 × 100,000 rupees) but had given them all away, to live as a *Sannyâsinî*. Nobody knew her age, she was believed to be at least a hundred years old, and yet she looked a prefect girl. Listening to these and similar stories, we reached the friend's house, and sent in our names, but had to wait a considerable time in the court in the centre of the spacious house. The master, we were told, was just performing his *Pûjâ* (morning prayers), and no one was allowed to disturb him. We had left the free-thought of the Roy's house to go back to the strict piety of India. At last our friend appeared, and we now set off to see the nun. We were taken up to the first floor, to a roomy but perfectly empty chamber. A simple carpet covered the whole floor. The saint appeared and I bowed, not daring however to shake hands with her. She was exceedingly simply but decently clad, her long black hair was worn loose, and fell over her shoulders to her feet, which were clad in stockings. In manner she was quiet and unassuming. Everything about her made the impression of a good hearted, motherly matron of about forty-five to fifty years of age. She spoke Sanscrit quite well, and among other questions I put I asked her which of the six philosophical systems was the best. She replied that they were all equally good, a remark which would surprise me less to-day than it did then. In a certain sense all six philosophical systems complete each other, forming one complete conception of the universe. The *Mîmânsa* stands in the ante-chamber of philosophy, treating only of ritual, and logically laying down all the dialectical pros and cons. The Vedânta is the metaphysics proper of India, the Sânkhyam only a realistic transformation of the Vedanta metaphysics as contained in the older Upanishads. The contrast is greatest between these two systems, without however destroying the inner relationship. The Yoga is the practical side of the Atman doctrine, not the moral side, for he who looks upon this world as an illusion is beyond good and evil, being rather a peculiar kind of technic, to enable one by penetration of one's own soul to get immediate hold of the Brahman, the Atman. With regard to the Nyâya and the Vaiseshikam, the former furnishes a generally accepted canon of logic, the latter a natural scientific classification of all that exists, divided into six categories.

The saint's answer to my question is therefore quite comprehensible from the unhistorical standpoint, the one all Indians hold. Equally unhistorical was the answer the centenarian gave me when I asked her age. "Na jnayate," (that is *not known*) was her simple reply.

It was now her turn to put questions, and her chief one was to what caste I belonged. As all non-Brahmanic Indians are categorically reckoned as among the caste of the Sûdras, the pariahs, I had previously declared myself to be a Sûdra when this question was put. I had however excited such painful surprise in my hearers that I afterwards always told them a pious fiction, in which I described myself as a Brahman, who, in consequence of a sin committed in a previous existence had sunk to the degree of a European, a Sûdra, but that I trusted in my next existence to be permitted to become a Brahman again. This little fiction, which generally excited much merriment I retailed for the benefit of the saint, but I had reckoned without my host. Scarcely had I explained that in a former birth I had been a Brahman when she interrupted me, and asked in a very severe tone how I knew that. I answered "Listen" and quoted some verses from Kâlidâsa's Sakuntalâ, which went to prove that I was right when I asserted that since first beginning to study Sanscrit I had felt so strongly attracted by it that I was fain to believe that I had spoken Sanscrit in a former existence, hence I must at one time have been a Brahman. This argument appeared to convince the good matron, and on my going on to describe how in consequence of some grave sin I had sunk to a Sûdra, a European, the deepest compassion could be read in her face. I continued "Now, after having visited India, having tarried in Benares, having seen you, oh, holy one, I dare hope that in my next existence I may again become a Brahman." The holy woman burst into tears, which as they rolled down her face and breast, she wiped with her hair.

At last our audience came to an end. The venerable woman bade us farewell, and when we reached the door a servant standing there presented us with a quantity of sweets, which were much in our way until we at last got rid of them by presenting them to the Roy children.

On the afternoon of the same day I went with Mr. Roy to see the well-known publisher of numerous Sanscrit texts, Jîvânanda Vidyâsâgara, who is, however, rather notorious than famous. We found him in the same position as on the picture adorning his edition, sitting cross-legged on a low, but exceedingly big, table, surrounded by books and manuscripts. His father Vâsaspatimisra, is the editor of an extremely comprehensive encyclopædiac Sanscrit Dictionary, published in four fat closely printed volumes. It is barely known in Europe, not being, so far as I know, quoted in Bohthlingk and Roth's Dictionary, though they frequently refer to the Cabdakalpadruma, a large parallel work, but which is not nearly so complete. Both these encyclopædias are extensively used in India, and in bringing out a new edition of either, the attempt is always made to profit by and outrival the other. A new edition of the Cabakalpadruma was just appearing, for which I subscribed, paying the small price of seventy rupees—all the succeeding numbers, down to the very last, have since duly reached me. I wanted to have the Vâsaspatyam as well, and only paid one hundred rupees for the four thick, well-bound volumes. On this occasion I learned from Jîvânanda how incredibly cheap bookbinding is in India, even the binding of very thick volumes can be reckoned in pence. I bought a quanity of other books in Jîvânanda's shop. The student must be warned of their frequent inaccuracies, but for want of better editions they do good service, the more so as the difficult texts are usually provided with a commentary written or compiled by Jîvânanda himself. As polyhistorian the man is not wanting in merit, but he possessed a corresponding supply of vanity: "I have spent," he told me, "more than 600,000 rupees on my editions; every day I get over 64 printed, and write as many as 40." I answered by telling him that we should value him more highly in Europe if he had less printed, and had that a little more correctly printed. His excuse was that he was often ill from overwork, and was then obliged to leave the work to strangers. At last we came to speak of Sanscrit verse-making, and he said: "I shall write down a verse for you, and I wager you will not be able to make sense of it, no matter how you turn it." He wrote down the verse, which is still somewhere among my papers, and all I said in reply was that in our country we more highly esteemed those who wrote verses comprehensible to all, than those who wrote verses understandable to none. We filled a big box chock-full of books, for which I paid the freight from Calcutta to Hamburg, something like seven rupees. The freight from Hamburg to Kiel came to the same amount, and there was besides a long bill for unloading, landing, customs-dues, &c. But if that were not so, what would the Hamburg agents and shipping firms do for a living?

We did not wish to leave Calcutta, without having been to see its celebrated Botanic Gardens. We had already planned to go there once before in the company of Frau Doctor Hörnle, whose husband was at that time Principal of the Mahomedan Madrasa College in Calcutta, but whose chief interest very naturally centred in Sanscrit. In the course of a very pleasant evening we spent at his house, he showed us the two Buddhistic manuscripts, medicinal in contents, dating from the 4th century, B. C., which had but recently been discovered at that time, and were exciting much interest on account of their great antiquity. That same evening an excursion to the Botanic Gardens had been fixed for the following day, but did not come off, owing to its having rained hard in the night, and the damp vegetable air of India being all too apt to bring on a touch of fever. Shortly before we left, however, we managed to get to the Gardens with the Roys. The gardens lie to the north of the town, on the other side of the Hughli, and the Roy's house being also in the north of Calcutta, we found we could save a long detour south, across the Hughli bridge, and then back north again, by taking a boat and rowing straight down stream to the Gardens. Our friend Mullik sent us a boat rowed by a dozen boatsmen in uniform, and so we rowed across the yellow waters of the Ganges in great style and landed at a little flight of steps leading straight to the finest part of these most extensive gardens. Immediately after entering, we turned down a long broad avenue, planted on either side with lofty palm-trees, all equal in size, variety and shape. The aspect was one of overwhelming beauty. Farther on too, wherever the eye pleased to rest it met with the most perfect display of all the splendour of the tropical vegetation. After passing through tastefully laid out shrubberies, flower-beds and creepers we arrived at the great sight of the gardens—the big Nyagrodha tree. This tree, the *ficus Indica,* whose Sanscrit name signifies "the tree that grows downward," lets its branches grow downwards till they happen to reach the ground, whereupon they take root and grow into new stems, so that in the end one tree multiplies into a forest. This, however, is a rare case, despite the frequency with which the Nyagrodha tree is met with both in gardens and along the roadsides. The branches mostly fail to reach the ground, and grow roots in the air, with the result that they wither away. A few Nyagrodha trees, however, and those are counted among the sights of India, have succeeded in taking root and forming a complex of tree-stems. The most celebrated of these trees is the one in the Caluctta Botanic Gardens. It is very difficult to get a clear idea of the whole, even when walking round it, and a photo can give no idea of it whatever. The parent stem, easily recognisable by its girth sends out its branches horizontally and from these branches fresh stems grow earthwards. A number of them have already attained no mean size, others are still in the process of being, and are supported in their downward growth by protective bamboo sheaths.

We must refrain from any further description of Calcutta's numerous sights, contenting ourselves with the mere mention of the Zoological Gardens, the the extensive Maidan, where we were wont to take our morning walk, till driven homewards by the sun, the Museum of Antiquities, the Eden Gardens with the Siamese Pagoda, the Museum of the Asiatic Society, a picture of which I had so often contemplated on the numbers of the *Bibliotheca Indica.* In the same way I am forced to omit the mention of much pleasant intercourse with natives of various ranks and classes. Mrs. Roy gave me a charmingly appropriate souvenir of Calcutta in the shape of a *Huggu* made out of a cocoa-nut, into which the smoke is introduced into the water from the top. The mouth is applied to a second hole in the upper part of the nut—the part containing no water. As the burning tobacco is balanced in a clay head, straight above the nut, care must be taken not to move the whole from its perpendicular position, and it is an exceedingly curious sight to see the smoker pressing mouth, head and neck to the nut at every puff. A little pipe, if added, would do away with all inconvenience, but the very fewest natives indulge in such luxury. The average smoker, who might be seen in Calcutta, sitting in the street in front of his hut, inhales the smoke straight from the hole bored in the cocoa-nut. The water-pipes used in Turkish countries are different, and elaborately furnished with glass receptacles and tubes. They are called Nargilehs, and the name is said to be of Persian origin. When however, I point out that Narikela means a cocoa-nut in Sanscrit, and that the principal part of an Indian water-pipe is mostly a real-cocoanut, we cannot be far wrong in assumiug the name and the custom to have originated in India, and to have been transplanted from there to more Western climes.

CHAPTER VII.

FROM CALCUTTA TO BOMBAY *via* ALLAHABAD.

IN the evening of February 8th our friend Roy accompanied us to the station, where a large circle of our Calcutta friends and acquaintances had assembled, to bid us good-bye. Our parting was unfortunately rather an uncomfortable affair, the train being a mail train, and consequently very full. An enormous crowd was surging up and down the platform. There was scarcely enough places even in the first-class, so I got my wife into the ladies' carriage, and managed to secure one side of a compartment for myself in another carriage, the company guaranteeing a bed to all first-class passengers. There was more room at one of the next stations, where two young Englishmen who had the top berths, got out. As the train was steaming in they got down from their berths in a most leisurely fashion and proceeded to dress. The train stopped, they were pulling on their boots and tying cravats. First signal for our start, they were putting on hats and shutting portmanteaux ;—second signal, and our train began to move,—out got one of the young men, and running alongside took the luggage, the other handed it out while most coolly looking about for something or other. The train was already going at some speed when the young fellow jumped down with unshaken phlegm, and got off without accident. The English have a certain foolhardiness, which however is seldom if ever attended by evil consequences, as they know exactly how much to risk.

Next morning our train stopped at Moghal Sarai, opposite Benares, and here Govind Dâs turned up to say how-do-you-do, and hastened, as before mentioned, to introduce Colonel Olcott to me. Our meeting was a short one, for they stayed behind; while I had to continue my journey I cast a last look of admiration at the sacred city, towering up in the morning light on the other side of the Ganges, and another less admiring glance at the revered head of the Theosophists, and his faithful adept, and on we went along the southern bank of the Ganges, till we reached Prayâga at 3 o'clock in the afternoon. The Mohammadans have done away with this ancient city's sacred name, calling it Allahabad instead, much as their brethren in the West have done with the Hagia Sophia, scratching out the angels' faces and painting in stars instead.

We got out and drove to Laurie's Hotel. I was just considering what steps to take to find Professor Thibaut, who had attended Weber's lectures on Sakuntalâ with me in 1866, when among other names I read that of Professor Thibaut and family in the hotel list. He was living in the hotel with his wife and two children, while looking out for a suitable house, and attending to his duties at the Sanscrit College in Allahabad. Strangely enough, though a

German by birth, he taught English there, Sanscrit lying in the hands of his Principal, Gough. Both are notable savants in the province of Indian Philology, but I can recognise in neither any deeper insight into the philosophy of the Indians, despite their efforts. In personal appearance they presented a striking contrast: Mr. Gough, a tall, stout Englishman, always pleasant, smiling, jovial; Thibaut, grave, very reserved in bearing. Thibaut told me he had to teach four hours a day, so that though Professors in India would appear to have higher salaries, they have to work harder for them than their German colleagues.

I hastened to pay my visit to the Thibaut's before we met at dinner, so we sat down to that meal at a table to ourselves. Our opinions concerning India differed widely; Thibaut warmly praised the English supremacy, which had conferred order and civilization upon the land. He was no enthusiastic admirer of the scenery either. He preferred Europe because in India, though garden flowers were to be met with, there were no wild flowers, though he cannot be supposed to have meant literally what he said, for if there are no wild flowers how can there be garden flowers? Does he mean to imply that the English were the first to introduce garden flowers, and must we suppose that the rain of flowers so frequently mentioned in ancient Indian poetry came from some other planet? I had still greater difficulty in getting on with Mrs. Thibaut, she was so sharp and contemptuous in speaking of the natives that I felt obliged to contradict her, on the strength of my own personal experiences, rather more energetically than is my wont in a discussion with a member of the fair sex.

The coolness of our relations rendered me all the more sensible to the warmth with which the Indians here too made me welcome. Scarcely had our arrival been bruited abroad than half a dozen visitors appeared the very first evening, almost before dinner was over. As we had only one day to spend at Allahabad an extremely heavy programme was arranged for the following day. Our first visit was of course to be paid to the sacred meeting of the Gangâ and the Yamunâ, then we were to see the other sights, and towards evening I agreed to lecture on the philosophy of the Vedanta, a young advocate Roshan Lâl undertaking to have the invitations printed and circulated, as indeed he was at pains to make all further arrangements. Krishna Joshin had offered to fetch us early next morning with a carriage, and our start was so hurried a one that I left all my money, a bundle of rupee notes, under my pillow. I insisted on driving back for my servant Purân, which was only a pretext for geting my bundle, and by taking both with me ensure the integrity of either. Purân had already made the beds, and my bundle was still lying under the pillow, seemingly as I had left it. I had to conclude that either Purân was really very honest, or that he was in the habit of airing his beds very badly. Much relieved we drove through the big populous city, across the Yamunâ, and at last came to Prayâga, "the sacrificial spot," also known as Trivenî, *i. e.*, the triple lock as three rivers here meet and mingle their waters, the Gangâ and the Yamunâ, the heavenly Gangâ, which exists in the imagination only, forming the third. The last tongue of land jutting out between the two rivers is neither tilled nor inhabited, but it has nothing of the awe-inspiring sublimity with which Delphi or Lake Herta inspires one. The tendency of the Indians to combine religion and sport is here very striking. A motley merry crowd assembles on Prayâga at the hour of the morning bath. Some are seen merrily splashing in the water, others drying their clothes on the shore, all chatting, laughing and joking. Booths of all kinds are to be seen, there is no dearth of flowers and sweets; beggars and jugglers force a path for themselves through the festive crowd, and their harvest is no stinted one. We got into one of the numerous boats and had ourselves rowed to the spot where the blue waters of the Yamunâ mingle with the yellow waves of the Gangâ, to flow on in one muddy current. The gay groups on the shores, the sunny Indian landscape, crowned by the tall-towered town in the distance, might have been a fit spectacle for gods. But alas! no one can experience such a wealth of impression as it was our lot to enjoy in the course of our travels without suffering a species of satiety.

We made our way back by way of the fort, stopping to examine the famous pillar which is adorned with the edicts of King Asoka, the patron of Buddhism, but at the same time a king tolerant of all religions. Various inscriptions have been added at a later date. Close by, we went down into a vault to view the miraculous *Akshaya Bata*, the "eternal fig tree", which grows in a cellar-like space, to which neither air nor light has free access, and yet the fig tree does not perish, a veritable miracle—unless it should prove that a little assistance is lent from time to time.

We spent the rest of the forenoon in seeing the town and in paying visits. Immediately after tiffin a number of Pandits took possession of me and stayed till four o'clock, when Roshan Lâl appeared to take me to tea at his house and then to the lecture. The spacious hall took some time to fill, while I sat enthroned at my desk between two candelabra, supremely oblivious of the curious looks which the audience were bestowing upon me, and hastily disposing in my mind the beginning, middle and end of my lecture. I had had no time for any preparation, but I was so thoroughly familiar with my subject, both in its general structure and details, that I had no hesitation in trusting to the inspiration of the moment. Nor did it leave me in the lurch. When the hall was quite full I had doors, windows and shutters closed, and developed the Vedânta in its monistic Advaita form, with all the fire and emphasis of one convinced. The Advaita form is the only one that can be taken seriously, and, careless of the standpoint my audience might assume, I characterized all the other forms, the theistic one in particular, as empirical degenerations. Here again I was asked with genuine Indian *naivete* to be kind enough to repeat my lecture in Sanscrit, for the benefit of those who did not understand English. I did so briefly, and now the debate followed, which afforded a striking proof of the gravity and enthusiasm with which philosophy is studied in India, which might well put Europe to shame. Some spoke English, others Sanscrit, others again expressing themselves in Hindi. I met with expressions not only of assent, but also of earnest contradiction, especially on the part of those who cannot content themselves with an impersonal Brahman, and who refuse to consider his personification as Isvara merely as a compromise with the human understanding, limited as it is to empirical views. Those again were contradicted by others among the audience, and so the war of opinions waged fiercely until at last all united in an enthusiastic vote of thanks for the lecture I had given them. One of the speakers went into ecstasies in my praise and reached a climax in his concluding words: "*dhanyo si, dhanyo si, dhanyo si,*" *i. e.*, you are a blessed being. Another, who spoke English, referred to my wife, who was seated beside me, and while putting me up as an ideal to men, and my wife as a model to women, went so far as to formulate the wish, "May all Indian men strive to emulate Professor Deussen, all Indian women Mrs. Deussen!" The time had come to close the meeting. We were conveyed in triumph to our hotel and went to bed with the consciousness of having spent a most interesting day.

I had expressed a wish to hear Indian music, and next morning Krishna Joshin got up a little concert for us. Early in the morning he and his son came to fetch us. We had plenty to see and marvel at on our way, a spacious reading-room amongst other things, got up and kept up by voluntary contributions, in which any person was free to read books, magazines and papers gratis all day long. I had no hesitation in expressing the highest appreciation of the whole institute, and readily agreed to write a Sanscrit remark to that effect in the Visitors' book. We now came upon our musicians, who had encamped in a shady spot in the open air, and who performed several pieces of music after our arrival. In addition to what I have already said of Indian music I should only like to add that it gains with every time it is heard. The melody is governed by rhythm only, and has no harmonious accompaniment, ascending rapidly from the key-note to the 7th and octave, where it rocks hither and thither in passionate minor tones, like a ball kept aloft on the jet of a fountain, till it descends again to the melody of the key-note, a phantastic music that penetrates the very soul. I was particularly interested in examining the instruments and having them explained; some of them are stringed instruments, such as the Vînâ, which reproduces the melody, others are instruments of a cymbal-like nature, the Mridanga, for instance, serving to accentuate the rhythm.

We spent the rest of the morning in going to see a school, where the Rig Veda was specially taught. The school was situated in a dirty, neglected quarter of the native town, and presented no very attractive appearance. But it was all the more interesting to me to hear the pupils reciting the Rig Veda, which has been almast entirely relegated to the background in India; they did so while keeping time with their hands to the accents.

We were loath to leave Allahabad, a place in which we had had an opportunity of experiencing Indian warmth and European indifference in such close proximity to each other. The last half-hour at the station was particularly enjoyable, as a large number of our newly acquired friends put in an appearance. I say friends advisedly, for short though our acquaintance was, we spoke and parted with as much cordiality as if we had known each other for years.

After leaving Allahabad the train leaves the valley of the Ganges in a southerly direction, and a journey of forty hours brings the traveller to Bombay. We could not however make up our minds to return to Bombay, without having gone to see a place which lies somewhat off the beaten track, and is hence seldom visited by Europeans, though well worth a visit. It is the ancient royal city of Ujjayinî, situated up in the Vindhya mountains, and famed as the birthplace of India's greatest poet, Kâlidâsa. His spirit seemed to beckon us, repeating the verses of the Meghadûta:

> "Though northward bound ye may not tarry,
> Obey the best, not keep aloof,
> To Ujjayini's towers hasten,
> And taste of joy beneath their roof."

Our destination did not happen to be our northern home, but Bombay and the South of India, but just on that account we had to travel quite a distance north on a branch line up the Vindhya, if we wished to tarry for a short time in the atmosphere of the town, which must have once been resplendent in all the glories so glowingly described by Kâlidâsa. After travelling about twenty hours we got from Allahabad to Khandwa, which lies about half way between Allahabad and Bombay, and here the narrow gauge Vindhya line branches off to the north. We got out of the Bombay train about noon and lunched in the station refreshment room. We could scarcely eat anything however, so great was the heat, though we were not more than twenty hours' railway journey to the south of Allahabad. We comforted ourselves with the thought that we should soon be back in the north in a cooler mountain district, got into a small carriage of the branch railway, fortunately having it to ourselves all the way, and off we went north. The Narmadâ, which we had to cross, presented a most picturesque sight on the south slope of the Vindhya hills, forcing a way for itself over projecting rocks and boulders, its rushing floods dividing here and there to surmount some obstacle, only to unite again. This has caused Kâlidâsa to compare it to the ornamentation (*bhuti*) applied to the trunk of an elephant by dividing it into squares (*bhakti-chedais*). (Cp. Meghaduta 19.) We slowly and gradually steamed up the Vindhya, until after passing the garrison of Mhow we soon reached Indore, the residence of the Holkar, where we were to spend the night.

There is no hotel in Indore, and the Dak Bungalow is at some distance from the station. Under these circumstances we preferred to take possession of the Ladies' Waiting Room, and had our beds made up there. Unfortunately, the station boasted of no refreshment room, and in order to get some supper we were obliged to go to the Dak Bungalow, with a youth as a guide, who also guided us back. The matter was less inconvenient next morning when we combined our breakfast at the Dak Bungalow with an inspection of the town. We made the acquaintance of a young Parsee, a commercial traveller, and with that forwardness in which the Parsees so strongly differ from the Hindus, he actually asked me to send him a German Primer on my return to Germany. I contented myself with giving him a few titles, and advising him to have recourse to a bookseller.

Our morning was taken up with a cursory inspection of the town, the market-place, the Blue Palace, the Lal Bagh, public gardens containing wild beasts. On our walk I saw something quite familiar to me from Indian fairy-tales, but which I had never witnessed, a fight between two rams. As if at a word of command the animals rose on their hind legs and battered their heads so violently against each other that only the tremendous thickness of their skulls can have preserved them from injury. They kept on repeating this manœuvre over and over again, most phlegmatically and without a trace of passion, almost as if it was a kind of game for them.

About 10 A. M. we left Indore, got out at the next station, and by making use of a branch of the branch line got to Ujjayinī about mid-day. The little station and the adjoining Dak Bungalow are both situated outside the town. Not half a minute's distance from it lies modern Ujjayinī, surrounded by a well-preserved, daintily-built mediæval wall, with towers, battlements and gates. Ujjayinī has a population of 33,000 inhabitants, and boasts of only three European families, the governor's, the tax-collector's, and an engineer's; hence, the town is thoroughly Indian and has absolutely no European comforts. Finding it less hot in the hills than in the plain, we set out at haphazard for a walk through the town, starting from the north gate beside the station, and proceeding along the principal street to the south gate. Knowing nobody and having no letters of introduction we asked our way to the College, and managed to get speech of the Principal. We got rather a cool reception at first, but I was by this time no novice at finding the way to an Indian's heart. One Sanscrit scholar after another was sent for, and by the time half an hour had elapsed a goodly company had been got together and the conversation was an animated one. We arranged to meet at the Dak Bungalow in the evening, and in the meantime a young teacher was told off to show us about the town. Our first visit was to the Mahâkâla Temple, situated close by and visible from afar owing to the brightness of its walls; it is, of course, not the one extolled by Kâlidâsa, which was afterwards destroyed, but it is said to have been built upon the ancient site. The old measurements are even said to have been discovered on old drawings, and the temple re-built in exact accordance with them. The tower-like building is topped by a statue of Siva with a forest of arms, just as Kâlidâsa describes it. Should the temple really occupy the old site, it must in that case have been fully half an hour distant from the city, separated from it perhaps by gardens, for ancient Ujjayinî, which we had still to see, did not occupy the site of the present town, but lay at some little distance to the north. We were not admitted to the subterranean part of the temple, but were assured that there was nothing to see in it except a big stone Lingam, a symbol of Siva. Not far from the temple and the modern town flows the much-famed Siprâ, which also washes the walls of the ancient city. It was a noble river even in the month of February as broad as the Moselle at Coblentz, but not very deep, as we saw next day, when our elephant waded through it. I do not remember having seen a bridge. Farther down, at ancient Ujjayinî people cross in a ferry. We strolled along the height between the town and the river, reaching the bungalow safely about nightfall, to find our acquaintances of the afternoon, and a number of others, waiting. Fortunately, we happened to be the only guests, so one of the two rooms in the one-storied house could be arranged as our bed-room, while we received our visitors in the other. It is impossible to entertain such visitors in India as no one will either eat or drink except with those of his own caste. However they accepted, and heartily enjoyed my cigars. I ordered supper. It turned out that we could have the usual pan-cakes, but that there was no bread. My wife insisted upon having bread, as she could not eat the stuff. I gave orders to send to the town for bread. In vain. I was assured on all sides that there was no bread to be had in the town. "If you want bread," said one bright intelligence, "You must write to Indore for it, and it can be here to-morrow." Another proposed to write to the Governor and ask him for a loaf. "But I do not know the Governor," I said. "No matter," was the reply, "it is sufficient introduction to be a European. And how do you intend to see the town and the surroundings without having recourse to the Governor?" "I shall hire a carriage and drive." "A carriage? We have nothing but ox-carts in Ujjayinî." "No," said the smartest of those present, "Take my advice, write to Sir Michael Filose, the Governor, and ask him to let you have a guide and a vehicle for to-morrow. He will in all probability send you an elephant. The Governor lives at about twenty minute's distance from here. The messenger can be back with the answer within the hour."

The advice seemed good and I wrote accordingly adding a polite request for some bread. The answer could not have been more polite and obliging. At seven o'clock an elephant with an experienced guide was to be at our door. We were advised, the better to see everything, to arrange to stay two days, and were invited to dine with the Governor the following evening. A carriage would be sent to fetch us. The messenger brought back a loaf, and a dainty basket containing butter and fruit.

A fine elephant with his driver was at our door next morning at 7 A. M. The Governor had sent us one of his Secretaries to act as guide. His name was Abdul; we were exceedingly well-informed, and for a Mohammadan was exceptionally modest and full of tact. We were much less edified by the young Hindu teacher, Vinâyaka, who had been our guide the day before, and whom we had invited to occupy the fourth seat on the elephant, as a treat. We kept meeting little girls and old women, who all made more or less deep obeisances, some of them even throwing themselves flat on the ground. "This homage," Vinâyaka explained' "is not for you, but for the elephant. These ignorant people have been trained to do honour to every image of Ganesa, the god with the elephant's head. If they happen to meet a real elephant, something of a rarity in our town, they mechanically bow down before it, without stopping to reflect."

Our first and most important ride was to the ancient site of Ujjayinî. It lies about half an hour's distance to the north of the present town on the Siprâ, where the river makes a magnificent bend to the north-east, flowing round a hilly district on which the old town lay. Long straight lines can still be distinctly traced upon the hills, evidently the remains of what were once streets. "Every time it rains," said Abdul, "the water washes down coins and other relics out of the old town. It would be well worth while to undertake excavations, but the Holkar of Indore, who owns the land takes no interest in these things." "Why," I asked, "did the people desert the fine old site and move further south into the plain?" "Nobody knows," said Abdul, "some say in consequence of an outbreak of the plague, others that an earthquake destroyed the old town." "Is there none of it left?" "One solitary house. I shall take you there to see it. The people call it the house of the poet Bhartrihari." "But what is this," I exclaimed, "what are all these monuments so neatly built of stones, and what do the neat little feet mean carved on them?" "These monuments mark the place where a widow has had herself burnt alive with her husband's corpse." "A Sâti," I concluded, "or rather as the English say in their jargon, Suttee." The word Sâti signifies "being," the good one, *i.e.*, the wife who follows her husband even in death. It also means the act of being burnt as a widow, and, lastly, the spot where such a cremation has taken place.

We strolled on over the site of ancient Ujjayinî, and everywhere in the grass and shrub-covered soil we noticed peculiar formations which offered a remunerative vista for future excavations, and afforded our imagination ample scope. We got to the top of an eminence with a fine view of the Siprâ flowing below, and here stood the solitary house that some mere chance has spared, and which bears the name of the house of Bartrihari for no apparent reason. It may well have been one of the palaces which Kâlidâsa describes, with a flat roof, spacious court, terraces with a fine prospect, and the whole surrounded and protected by a wall, still in a state of good preservation. We entered the court by a doorway, coped by a mighty stone. A tree forcing its way upward, had split it in two, but the two pieces still stood leaning against each other, and thus preventing each other from falling. From the court we had a magnificent view of the Siprâ winding below and the country beyond the river. Judging by its situation, the house must evidently have been one of the finest in the town, a hypothesis confirmed by its various stories, which are still partially preserved; one of them, half buried by the earth which has given way, makes the impression of a cellar, but the story above gives a good idea of the well-to-do dwellings of ancient India. The whole story consisted of one single hall, long and broad, but exceedingly low. The ceiling was supported by a quantity of pillars, neatly hewn out of stone, scarcely exceeding a man in height. It was just possible to stand and walk upright. These low ceilings may have been intended to ensure a cooler atmosphere. I was strongly reminded of the old house we had seen at Mahâvan near Mathurâ, the one in which Krishna is said to have spent his boyhood. There too, the low ceiling was supported by pillars, to one of which his foster-mother used to fasten the young god when he was naughty.

The sun getting ever higher warned us not to delay. We got up on to our elephant again, left the deserted site of a mighty past and made our way across well-tilled fields, back to the new town, the streets of which were by this time so busy that we had some difficulty in passing. The elephant appeared to be accustomed to have every one move out of his way. He kept stolidly marching on not holding it beneath his dignity to exact a tribute from the passing carts. He ended by taking up in his trunk a whole sheaf of canes from a cart that passed laden with them. This he held broadside in his trunk, blocking up nearly the whole of the street. "What is he going to do with it," I asked Abdul, "You will soon see," he said, and the elephant there and then began to loosen the bundle with mouth and trunk, while continuing his march, and proceeded to eat one cane after the other with placid enjoyment. The elephant was most careful in the choice of his road. When wading across the Siprâ with us he would not advance a single step without having first assured himself of the bottom of the river, by groping about. We had gone to see some ponds in a part of the town as yet but sparsely built upon. One of these ponds bears the name of Gandhavâti, as in Kâlidâsa. We wanted to go on from here straight across a hollow, to climb the hill in the heart of the town and get a view of the entire surroundings. The driver was directing the elephant across this meadow, when the animal's foot sank at the first step more than half a yard into the soil. He quickly got out of his dangerous position, and we were much amused at the tremendous hole the elephant's foot had made.

We spent two days on our elephant in Abdul's pleasant company, viewing the ancient royal city and its surroundings. We went to the Observatory, so famous in the days of yore, and of which only the walls are left standing; went to Kalideh with its water-pipes and its ruins of palatial buildings, returning highly satisfied on the second day to dress for dinner at Sir Michael Filose's. The carriage was there for us at the appointed hour and took us to the Governor's country-house, situated at some distance from the town. The Governor was an Italian by birth, but so thoroughly Anglicised, that with his imposing figure and white hair he in no way differed from an old English gentleman. There were some grown-up daughters, and relatives present, as well as a Roman Catholic priest, Padre Pio, who was travelling about showing the plans and collecting the money for the creation of a Roman Catholic Church at Gwalior. We went to table, where the Padre said grace. I noticed that the inmates of the house were all strict Catholics. The lady I took in to table had only just returned from Italy, and I could feel how pleased she was when I spoke Italian with her. The Filoses, who have lived in India for generations, seem to have given up using Italian altogether. The conversation was animated, the prevailing spirits excellent. We were standing about after dinner chatting in a most lively fashion when the Padre began to say good-bye, as he wanted to catch the night train to Gwalior. To prevent the Governor's having to send his carriage twice on such a long drive, I decided to say good-bye too, and was just addressing a few kind words of farewell to the Governor, when the whole party suddenly dropped upon their knees. I retreated thunderstruck, and looked on respectfully from the background, while the Padre blessed those present. We then said good-bye, with best thanks for the kindness shown us, and drove with Padre Pio to the Bungalow; there being still an hour left till the train was due, the Padre smoked one or two of my cigars while explaining his Church plans to me. He refused however to accept any cigars for his journey, and left us when he heard the train in the distance, whereupon we went to bed.

We had arranged to leave at 10 o'clock next morning. Several acquaintances were at the station, including Abdul, who wanted to show me some of his curiosities. As I did not dare to offer him money I made him a present of a small pocket atlas, which can be bought in London in a prettily got-up edition for about half-a-crown. I have rarely seen anyone so delighted as Abdul was with this little present, which may, it is true, be a great rarity in Ujjayinî.

A long journey from Ujjayinî to Bombay now

followed, lasting the night and the whole of the following day with but trifling halts. We went down the Vindhya, past Indore, across the Narmadâ to Khandwa, where we caught the night train, passed the famous Nasik next day, and in the course of the afternoon got into the highly romantic highlands of the Western Ghauts consisting of imposing mountain ranges, which form a kind of rampart on the west side of the table-land of the Deccan. It is no easy task for the train to make its way down from these heights to Bombay. There are sections where the train runs backwards and forwards in a succession of zigzags, there are tunnels, bridges and bold curves galore, and all the time you have the most magnificent views of the mountains, plain and sea. About 9 o'clock that evening, after a splendid trip of more than two months, we steamed into Bombay, where there was nobody to meet us. We took a carriage, which like everything else in Bombay is strikingly more elegant and better than what Calcutta can afford, and drove straight to Tribhuvandâs', whom we had promised to help his Cosmopolitan into fashion, by going to stay there. No preparations having been made he put us up for the night in a modest apartment in his splendid palace.

Tribhuvandâs had inherited the wealth, if not the understanding, of his father, Sir Mangaldâs, a man of eminent and recognised merit. Being a true Vaisya, Tribhuvândas was intent upon increasing his wealth to the utmost. He was most obliging and good-natured, and his vanity, no mean quantity, was flattered even when he was made a butt, and he afforded considerable opportunity for so doing. In Girgaum Road, to the north of the town, he owned a palatial residence, with a splendid garden, in which grew lotus-flowers, betel-plants, and many other rare shrubs. At the foot of the big garden there was a second house, which our friends the four brothers Nazar had rented. We had made Tribhuvandâs' acquaintance through them, and spent many a delightful evening with him and his family in the cool, spacious hall of his palace, chatting, joking and making music. A big piece of property on the opposite side of the Girgaum Road belonged to Tribhuvandâs too. In a secluded corner of it he had put up a public-house for workmen, having established his hobby, the Cosmopolitan Club, in the principal building. It was intended, as the name implies, to satisfy the requirements of all nations. Vegetarian meals could be served in Hindu fashion, or European ones with meat and intoxicating beverages, and a number of Indians with a taste for European comfort were in the habit of meeting at the Club every day for meals. Tribhuvandâs did all he could to get Europeans to come to his Club, and we had allowed ourselves to be persuaded into going there, partly to get closer to Indians and Indian life than had been possible on the terrace of the Esplanade Hotel. We could choose what rooms we liked, and change as often as we liked. Being but simply furnished, three rupees a day was ample payment for us both, and as we were at liberty to make ourselves thoroughly at home in the big empty rooms of the first story, we enjoyed perfect quiet and peace—a rare thing in Bombay. We stood badly in need of it too, for I had promised the venerable and amiable Javerilâl Umiashankar, Secretary to the Asiatic Society, to lecture before the Society on the 25th of February, and I had determined to have my lecture printed, and leave it as a legacy to India. It has indeed done service there, having not only appeared as a pamphlet in English, which was fully reviewed in the chief papers, but having been widely circulated throughout India in Marathi, Guzarati, Bengali and various other translations. In the introduction I took a short glance at the present state of philosophy in India, and then gave a brief and concise sketch of the sole philosophy of India worthy of serious consideration, the Advaita doctrine of the oldest Upanishads, and of their great interpreter Sankara, (born 788, exactly one thousand years before the birth of Schopenhauer, with whom he is so closely allied in spirit). I did not omit to draw the attention of my hearers to the deep inner correspondence between this doctrine and the philosophy of Kant and Schopenhauer as well as the elements of Christianity, exhorting the Indians in conclusion to hold fast the Vedânta as the form accorded them of the one universal philosophical truth.

The working out of this lecture, as well as the printing of it, occupied my friends as well as myself, for the following days, and when the 25th arrived I was able not only to lecture on the thoughts I have just exposed, before a numerous audience, but to distribute the printed pamphlets among those present and to send copies to all our friends in India.

The lecture has been appended to this book, and is preceded by a few verses of farewell to the many friends I made in India.

Among the many experiences that were crowded into the last days of our stay in Bombay, I must not forget a wedding, to which one of our Hindu friends invited us. It has already been said, that in many of the castes all girls must be married before completing their eleventh year. When the date is at hand the girl's father has a look at the eligible boys, those belonging to his own caste only of course; rank, position and wealth being important points for consideration. Should the parents on both sides feel inclined for the match, the Brahmans are asked for advice, and they generally ask for the children's horoscopes to be brought them. Just as every child in our country is provided with a certificate of baptism, every Indian child has its horoscope drawn at a very early age. It consists of a very long roll of paper, covered with figures, signs and Sanscrit verses. It costs ten rupees to have such a document drawn up; some people were most anxious to draw up our horoscopes for us, but we had no curiosity to read our fortunes in the stars.

When a marriage is under discussion the Brahmans compare the children's horoscopes. If they are favourable to the union, the day, hour, and minute of the wedding are calculated from them, the result being often most inconvenient for the guests invited, who may have to wait all night, if the wedding happens to be fixed for three or four o'clock in the morning. We were more lucky however, for the horoscopes had decreed that the wedding was to take place at 7-53 A.M. Shortly after six o'clock a distinguished gathering assembled in the house of the bride's father. We were invited to step into the court where the ceremony took place behind a grating, so that we were able to see everything very well. The preparations were the most lengthy. First, the bride, then the bridegroom was the object round whom the ceremonies turned; sometimes the parents addressed them, sometimes it was a Brahman who murmured texts and verses over them. Meantime, cocoa-nuts had been distributed among the guests, and we accepted some too to avoid appearing rude. The hour for the marriage was rapidly approaching, everybody was watching the time; ten minutes more; five minutes—at last the time had come. A carpet was spread like a curtain inside the grating. On one side appeared the father with the son, on the other, the father with the daughter, each parent holding his offspring by the hand, the children being prevented by the curtain from seeing each other. The moment had arrived. When it was exactly fifty-three minutes past seven the children's hands were joined above the curtain, the curtain fell and the little couple was united for life. Congratulations, embraces, and general emotions followed, as with us. Then the merry-making began.

All night long feasting went on, the men being entertained in one room, the women in another, while in a third room the dancing girls performed the antics described elsewhere.

One of the men, whom friend Atmarâm took us to see during these last days in Bombay, was the well-known Sanscrit scholar, Judge Telang, one of the few natives drawing one of the exorbitant salaries generally reserved for European officials in India. We met him early one morning in the study of his elegant house, dressed in the native costume, surrounded by books and papers. We had an interesting conversation on scientific topics, and at the close of our visit he took us over his house. Far more striking than any of the splendid halls and chambers was a quiet recess, in which stood a number of idols, before which lay a number of fresh-cut flowers. I could not refrain from expressing my amazement that a philosophical and cultured man of Mr. Telang's standing should attach any importance to such things. "It is done for the sake of the women in my household," he made answer. "Every morning a Brahman comes here, says a prayer or two and puts down the fresh flowers, getting a small sum in return for this every month." We walked to the door, noticing some female figures behind a column as we passed, gazing at us with great curiosity. I thought they were servants, but heard afterwards from Atmarâm that they were the Judge's mother and wife. As my wife had accompanied me we felt it would only have been right for her to have been taken to see the ladies of the house, but Indian women are exceedingly shy of coming in contact with Europeans, as we have already had occasion to remark. This timidity will not disappear until the religious and national prejudices have been successfully overcome by an improvement in the girls' schools, and in particular by inducing the women to learn English. We had already seen at the Roy's in Calcutta how pleasant and stimulating intercourse with Indian women can be under these circumstances.

We paid a farewell visit too, to Professor Peterson, who is in the habit of changing his place of residence three times a year; during the hot season he goes with his family to the Hills, during the rainy season he has a house in town, and during the winter he lives in a tent. Such tents are set up on a great meadow far from the noise and dust of the town, and can be hired just as you hire a house. These tents have doors, drawing-rooms, bed-rooms, and other apartments, exactly like a house, and cannot be said to be inferior to the town residences either in size or elegance. The turf is covered with a carpet, the walls are hung with mirrors and pictures; there are hanging lamps, tables, sofas, chairs, beds, and other household articles without exception. A watchman is there to guard against thieves, and sometimes you find quite a number of tents together forming quite a little street. The whole system of living in tents is a very healthy and pleasant one, but it is only possible to adopt it in such a climate as Bombay, where there is neither cold nor rain, and a mere minimum of rain to be reckoned with during the course of the winter.

CHAPTER VIII.

FROM BOMBAY TO MADRAS AND CEYLON.

THE day of our departure kept getting nearer and nearer. We had got safely over the various farewell feasts given in our honour by the members of the Cosmopolitan Club, by Prince Baldevi, by Mr. Chichgar in the Parsee Club, &c., &c. All our farewell calls had been paid, our keepsakes bought, and our boxes packed. At an early hour dozens of friends and acquaintances had assembled in our spacious apartment, and looked on while we breakfasted. Tribhuvandâs pocketed a long row of rupees with a smile of satisfaction, and, jokingly promising to carry the name and fame of his Cosmopolitan Club throughout the realms of Europe, we got into our carriage and drove off to the palatial-looking Victoria Station, where the number of those who had come to see us off was further increased. There was literally no end to the good-byes, and a theosophistically-minded Parsee youth, called Ardeshir, *i.e.*, Artaxerxes, actually travelled with us for a short distance to hear my opinion anent theosophy. I could only repeat what I had said on many previous occasions. "You Theosophists," I said," acknowledge three principal aims: 1. You strive after a revival of the glorious traditions of antiquity, a praiseworthy ambition, only it must be undertaken by people who understand something, and not be left to people who are entirely ignorant. 2. You aspire to a common brotherhood of all humanity, an object all people ought heartily to concur in. 3. You would penetrate the most hidden depths of the human soul, as your programme expresses it. This last named point ruins your whole cause, opening the doors, as it does, to swindles, deception and all kinds of cheating. There are indeed depths of the human soul which have hitherto remained impenetrable; somnambulism, prophetic dreams and second sight are met with, though less frequently than is generally believed. To avoid falling into errors, however, in inquiring into these matters, we need men who so far do not exist, men with a thorough knowledge of natural science, of medicine in particular, and who are intimately familiar with true philosohpy, by which I mean the philosophy of Kant and Schopenhauer.

While we were talking on these matters the train had been rushing across the plain which separates Bombay from the Western Ghaut Mountains. The Parsee youth took leave of us, and we were able now to turn our attention to the scenery. The line, a marvel of modern railway engineering, kept rising higher and higher, affording an extensive and magnificent view over the green plain, the handsome city, and the wide ocean, till the hills shut off the view as if a curtain had been suddenly dropped, and the train reached Poona, situated upon the table-land. The younger Apte, whose uncle in Bombay had furnished us with introductions, was at the station to meet us. The uncle, since deceased, was a very rich and exceedingly pious old man. He had founded an Institute in Poona, the Anandâsrama (hermitage of bliss), which collects valuable manuscripts treating of religion and philosophy, and stores them in specially constructed fire-proof receptacles. In one of the numerous buildings of which the Institute is composed, the Anandâsrama-printing press has been set up which is kept busy printing the afore-mentioned works. The Institute comprises lecture rooms, and accommodation for the numerous persons engaged in the work, and provides poor scholars with free quarters for a specified time.

I had had an interview in Bombay with old Apte and his Pandits, in the course of which my breast and shoulders had been decorated with the customary wreaths of magnificent flowers, and at the close of which I had been presented with *attar* of roses and bouquets. My popularity too was no doubt somewhat due to the fact that I had subscribed to the whole Anandâsrama series in advance, the various numbers of which are still sent me regularly by the younger Apte, to whom the uncle left his whole business at his death. Shortly before his decease he had become a Sanyâsin, as so many pious Indians do in their old age; had taken a new name, as was customary, and was not cremated when he died, but buried, which is only done with *Sannyâsins* and very little children. The ceremony of cremation is dispensed with in either case, the children being looked upon as not yet being, the *Sannyâsins* as having ceased to be men. Apte was therefore interred amid the intellectual treasures he had stored up in Poona, and which are now gradually finding their way into all parts of the world, thanks to the enterprise of the old man's nephew.

It was this nephew who met us at the Poona Station and placed himself entirely at our service during our few days' stay in that city. He showed us the whole of the Anandâsrama Institute, called together a meeting of Pandits in our honour, took us to see the town, the gardens and the famous Sanga, *i.e.*, the meeting of the Muta and the Mula rivers. We used to end the day's wanderings at the Pârvatî Hill to the south of the town, where there was a temple to Durgâ or Pârvatî, sometimes called Gaurî too, the wife of Siva. From this hill we had a magnificent view of the city and its surroundings. Apte, a highly cultured and learned man, professed of course no religion but the Vedânta, but like Telang in Bombay, declared he was obliged to adhere to the worship of the gods on account of his family. All the images of the gods he looked upon as incarnations of the Atman, but he always took care not to confuse a mind that had not been able to rise to the idealism of this standpoint. I had the conviction here that those who think in India take the same free standpoint in matters of religious doctrine as the thinkers of Europe, but out of consideration for their families still adhere to the worship of the gods, in the same way that we still hold fast to the ceremonies of a Church marriage, baptism and burial, though free from all superstitious ideas.

Night had fallen when we at last left the Pârvatî Hill and set out on our way back to the town. The Holî, a popular festival was in full swing. Little bonfires, blazing brightly, had been lighted in the streets in front of the houses; figures either sat or stood round them, throwing flowers and seeds into the flames. Others strolled about in bands, indulging in all sorts of antics. It seemed a great joke to pelt one another with earth, and many of the people to protect their clothing, wore a kind of sack, which was plentifully bedaubed with clumps of soil. We were forcibly reminded of our own carnival or the Roman Saturnalia and whatever religious motive the feast may have been founded on, its present form seems to be due to the necessity all people feel at times for throwing off dull care and common sense, and becoming for the time being, children or fools—*dulce est desipere in loco.*

We, of course, did not omit to pay a visit to Professor Bhandarkar, who has done so much for Sanscrit, and we met with a kind reception in his charming and tastefully furnished villa. From Bombay I had sent him on my Vedânta lecture as a sort of visiting card. Our little talk very naturally reverted to philosophy, and in the course of a long evening walk I was delighted to notice the lively interest this intelligent and warm-hearted Indian took in the philosophy of Schopenhauer.

We passed three most pleasant days in Poona,

resting before the long hot twenty-eight hours' railway trip to Madras. It began at 3 A.M. one night, and after spending the whole of the following day and the following night in the train, we reached our destination at 5 A.M., having crossed from the Western sea to the Eastern ocean, from Malabar to Coromandel, leaving Central India for Southern India, in consequence of which we noticed a very considerable rise in the temperature on our short walk from the station to the Hotel.

The climate is very different and less auspicious than in Northern and Western India. The rainy season there falls in summer and is some protection from the intensely hot rays of the sun, which beat down upon the earth almost perpendicularly. Madras, on the other hand, is under the influence of the North-West winter monsoon, has its rainy season proper in winter, and the most intense tropical heat in summer, moderated only by the sea breeze.

Not only the climate, but the population, in colour, type and language, differs widely from that of the Northern and North-Western India. There the language and the population, in part at least, were Aryan in origin; here in the South-East and South of India, languages are spoken which have no connection with Sanscrit whatever. If you draw a line from Bombay to Orissa in a southerly direction, that line will be found to separate the seven Aryan languages from the four non-Aryan languages spoken in the South of India. The first of the seven is Hindustani, spoken throughout the plain of the Ganges from the Punjab to Bengal. It again consists of Hindi as spoken by the people, and Urdu, which is nothing but Hindi corrupted by the introduction of numbers of Persian and Arabian words. These intruders, which may be compared to French words in the English language contribute considerably to render Hindustani more difficult, pure Hindi on the other hand being very easy for anyone with a knowledge of Sanscrit, being really nothing more than a Sanscrit which has dropped the endings, supplying their places by particles. Under the Mahomedan conquerors the corrupt form of Hindustani came to be a kind of *lingua franca*, which is more or less understood throughout all India. Closely allied with the Hindi spoken in the valley of the Ganges is Bengali and Orissa. In the West, Pendschabi is spoken in the Punjab, Hindi along the Indus; Gujarati north of Bombay; Marathi to the north-east of Bombay beyond the plateau of the Deccan. Those are the seven Aryan languages of India, which stand in the same relation to Sanscrit as the Romanic languages do to Latin, and differ about as much as the last mentioned do from one another. On the other hand, the languages of the South have no points of resemblance with Sanscrit. They are: 1. Telegu, spoken on the East Coast of India between Orissa and Madras. 2. Tamil, spoken between Madras and Ceylon, where it comes in contact with Singalese, which is generally looked upon as an Aryan tongue; 3. Kanarese, and 4. Malayâlam. Twelve languages in all which are spoken to this day in India and Ceylon. We were in the country of Telugu when we got to Madras. The dusky-hued people in the native town, which the English have dubbed Black Town, and their language, made us feel great strangers ; we could make nothing of the single words we managed to catch. I was all the more glad to find an old acquaintance in Mr. Oppert, Professor of Sanscrit in Madras at that time. He was a bachelor and had a house of several stories to himself. He insisted on our going to stay with him, which we consented to do after having spent a bad night in the hotel, the heat being very great and our room very small. But we were to find no rest even in Oppert's house. He had invited a number of guests that evening and after they had left us, he conducted us into a fine big airy bed-room, where however the beds had no mosquito-nets. Mr. Oppert comforted us by pointing to the punkah over the beds. I had heard a good deal of the punkah-drawers, and decided to have one that night. The punkah-drawer gets about 6*d*. a night. He did not fall asleep over his task ; I neither required to squirt water nor throw boots at him, as some people do when the man falls asleep, and his employer wakes to find himself bathed in perspiration. I did not manage to sleep however, but spent the whole night fighting mosquitos which left us no peace, despite the punkah. Oppert was exceedingly kind to us, and was also an adept in his dealings with the Indian students. He went for walks with them, invited them to come and see him, and devoted himself to them in every way. He took me to his Sanscrit class, and left the entire management to me. It is an hour I shall not forget; in front of me sat about thirty dusky youths, hanging on my words and my eye could wander from the ruddy sand to the foaming surf, which sent a welcome breath of cool air through the wide-open windows.

Madras has a magnificent beach but no harbour, like all the rest of the Indian East Coast. One had been built at enormous expense by sinking huge masses of stone into the sea, but then a storm came and swept away all that had been done. A still stronger breakwater was on the point of being completed when we were there. Let us hope it may manage to defy the force of the storms.

When we were at Fort Saint George our attention was drawn to something very strange. I was looking out to sea through a telescope, when I saw two men drifting on a craft consisting of a few beams held together by a few cross-planks at about an hour's distance from the shore. Huge waves were breaking over them, the little craft now rose above, now sank beneath the waves. It looked more dangerous than it really was. So long as these amphibious individuals can stick to their raft they have nothing to fear, a constant bath being decidedly refreshing with the thermometer so high.

At the Fort in Madras I saw, amongst books and manuscripts, a copy of the Indian Gazetteer, consisting of a great many heavy volumes. It is an annual statistic report of all sorts of facts relating to each of the provinces. In this, as in so many other matters, the English administration must be considered a model to all others.

When in Madras I happened to hear that the Mahârâja of Vijayanagaram, a small kingdom on the East Coast to the South of Orissa, was staying at one of his palaces not far from the town. This man's name was familiar to me from the Oriental Congress, which had been held in London some six months previously. When the English Government, having defrayed the expenses of the first edition, refused to defray the expenses of the second edition of the Rig Veda Max Müller was publishing, the Mahârâja of Vijayanagaram came forward and did so. In his address at the Congress Max Müller explained, "This noble Prince has not only defrayed the entire expenses connected with the publishing of the work, but has placed a number of free copies at my disposal, so that anyone seriously engaged in the study of the Rig Veda may receive a gratis copy on applying to me." As the net price of the work is £ 8 this liberality made a deep impression on Max Müller's audience. I did not require to take advantage of the offer, as Max Müller had long before presented me with a copy, but I have repeatedly applied to Müller for a free copy for friends of mine of both sexes.

Great was my joy to hear that the Mahârâja was staying at his palace near Madras, as I had not hoped to meet him in India. After tiffin I took a carriage and drove out with my wife to the palace which stands in magnificent gardens. We had some difficulty in getting a gouty old Englishman to inform the Mahârâja of our arrival, but after waiting about half an hour a servant appeared and conducted us into the Mahârâja's presence. He was a refined-looking, delicate, retiring young man of distinguished bearing. I told him about the London Oriental Congress and how grateful we all feel to him. He listened with great interest and put a number of questions to me about my travels, while tea was served in silver cups. I spoke of my impressions, presented him with a copy of my Bombay lecture, at which he appeared touched, and at his request read him my "Farewell to India." We then said good-bye and drove back to Madras.

Instead of taking the steamer from Madras to Colombo, we preferred to travel by train to the most southerly point of the dearly-loved land, paying flying visits to the towns of Tanjore, Trichinopoly and Madura, with their temples and palaces. We were able to do so by travelling by night and spending the days in visiting the towns. The first night we got from Madras and Tanjore, where we did the sights, the great temple in particular, driving about in an ox-cart, the only vehicle procurable, on which we lay full length. Brahmanism has been imported into Southern India, and has here erected giant temples to its gods as if to protect them in the foreign land. These temples take up whole districts in the towns and are like well-guarded fortresses. The holy of holies, to which no European is admitted, is surrounded by as many as five and more ramparts containing the priests' dwellings and other offices. These ramparts are pierced by lofty arches called Gopuras, which taper into tall towers. Both the arches and the towers are studded with heaps of mythological figures, sculptured in relief, and many of the groups, which are coloured, are very beautiful.

Two hours' farther travelling brought us to Trichinopoly, where we went to see another giant temple with lofty Gopuras, and when it had got cooler we went on to an imposing rock overlooking the town, with rock-hewn pathways and praying shrines, topped by a temple. The view of the town, landscape and mountains was very fine, and we savoured it all the more in the consciousness that within twenty-four hours we should have to bid farewell to the sacred soil of India.

Another broken night's rest in the train and we reached Madura early in the morning. We engaged a guide to take us sight-seeing. As we partook of refreshments on the way we offered some to the man who politely declined them on the pretext that his high caste prohibited him from doing so. He took us to the famous Nyagrodha-tree which very nearly rivals the Calcutta one. After seeing the palace and the temple, with all their treasures we got into the train again at noon, on our way to the south point of India, where at Tuticorin we were to catch the Ceylon steamer. This steamer was to touch at Tuticorin on its way from Bombay at 6 P. M. Our train was due five minutes later, so we had wired to the steamer to wait for us. An employee of the shipping company was waiting for us at the station, who urged us to make haste as the ship was lying outside the harbour. "Have you got the steam-launch ready I wired for?" I asked. "Yes Sir." We hastened to the shore and found in place of the launch a common sailing-boat with no seats and no deck, but such very high bulwarks that we had to climb up every time we wanted to see over. It was getting dark, and in this wretched barge we were expected to make our way to the steamer, which lay too far out for us to see her. I was extremely angry at this, and insisted upon the employee going out with us as far as the steamer. My wife and our numerous pieces of baggage were carefully lowered on to the dirty floor of this miserable craft, we followed, and cowered down beside her and the voyage began. The wind was in our faces and we had to tack. The wind blew harder, the sea got rougher. My wife turned sea-sick and things became very uncomfortable. The short tropical twilight had been followed by pitch darkness. I kept climbing up the side of the boat to try and see the steamer's lights, but we seemed to be getting no nearer. Suddenly the man at the helm uttered an exclamation with a face of terror. "What did he say," I asked. "He says that there is no light on the wreck that lies on our course," was the answer. What would happen I wondered if we collided with it. "It would have been your last hour," said the captain of the steamer when I told him. At last we began to get nearer the steamer-lights and reached the vessel at 8 P. M. after a sail of two hours of anguish. The sea was so rough that it was not possible to let down the ship's ladder. Two of the ship's officers clambered down a rope-ladder and half shoved, half dragged my wife on deck, while our boat danced wildly alongside the ship. Our various boxes and bags were now pulled up on ropes, and I watched them hovering over the face of the waters with an anxious eye. If a lock gave way all the contents would be swallowed up by the sea. At last everything was on board. I swarmed up the rope-ladder, paid the men and the steamer began to move. It was a big luxurious steamer belonging to the Asiatic Society, a native line. There were not many passengers on board and most of them were natives. We got a good reception, had plenty to eat and drink, and were given a big clean airy cabin, in which we spent a comfortable night, the first after a considerable number of broken nights. Next morning we lay 'twixt the sea and sky. About noon the outline of Ceylon began to appear above the sea, and gradually got nearer this wonderful island, with its wealth of palm forests and its lofty mountains. We cast anchor about 3 P. M., and while getting out we read a big printed warning to travellers on the dangers of sunstroke. We were soon comfortably installed in a room in a good hotel. Full board per day is not charged as in India, so it was easy to see that the hotel expenses would be double those we had in India, as everything had to be paid for separately.

We ordered dinner and sent for two Jinrikshas. These are delightful little carts, quite elegantly turned out, with room for one person on a seat between two wheels; they are drawn, not by horses, but by a chocolate-coloured man, stark naked but for his turban and a loin-cloth. The institution is a Japanese one, as is the name, which signifies man-carriage. The Jinrikshas are nearly as fast as cabs, and very much cheaper. We wanted to pay a visit to a very old school-friend of mine, Mr. Philipp Freudenberg, the German Consul, who was a native of Westerwald like myself. Our parents had been friends, and we had often played together when children, though it was forty years since we had seen each other last (1853). Our two human horses trotted bravely on, and after a short drive through the villa-district of Colombo, with its fragrant gardens, we got to Freudenberg's house, which had a fine verandah and garden. There were lights on the verandah and we had scarcely sent in our cards when we heard a strong German voice say "At last!" Freudenberg, who had long been looking forwards to our visit, gave us the heartiest of welcomes. He was alone, his wife being in Germany with her four sons, and his brother being away on his honeymoon in the mountains. There was no saying 'no' to his hearty invitation to come and stay with him while we were in Colombo. I agreed to come the following day, but he insisted on our coming that very evening, so there was nothing for it but for me to return to the hotel, give up our rooms, and return bag and baggage at a pretty late hour to my friend's beautiful house, which was named Srinivesa, *i.e.*, the abode of Happiness. The whole of the first floor was placed at our disposal, and we thoroughly enjoyed the hospitality offered us in so well-appointed a house. An army of servants, with their long hair caught up Singalese fashion with a comb, waited on us at table; the most luscious of fruits, pine-apples, bananas and mangoes being served at the close of the repast. On our expressing our admiration at this lavish display Freudenberg said very modestly, "It is our usual desert."

But not alone for our material comfort did our kind host care. As far as his time permitted he drove about the town with us sight-seeing. I have a vivid recollection of the capital museum, the great Buddha Temple, with its colossal statue of a reclining Buddha and the splendid beach, where a refreshing breeze always blew. We paid a most interesting visit to our friend's large cocoa-nut oil factory. He took us through the store-room, in which the raw material was drying, in particular the fleshy pith between the wood-like shell and the juicy inside. We saw the machines for cutting, stamping, and rubbing the material until out of the mighty presses a broad stream of clear golden cocoa-nut oil came bubbling forth. In another part of the factory huge casks were being constructed, each to contain about 500 liters, which, when filled, were to be sent to all parts of the universe. My friend had a coffee business as well, before, but tea has now taken the place of coffee, ever since the coffee plantations in Ceylon have been so devastated by an insect, that coffee growing no longer pays.

We left our friend for a few days to go up to Kandy, the ancient capital of the island, situated in the mountains. The railway runs for some time through the dense palm-forests that skirt the coast, then begins to ascend, and reaches Kandy in about 5 hours. At one of the stations we stopped at, a man was offering cocoa-nuts for sale at a penny a piece. I bought one. The man knocked off the top part of the nut shell very cleverly, and I thus got a natural goblet containing a cooling beverage not unlike a weak lemonade in taste. Towards evening we arrived at Kandy, which is charmingly situated amid wooded mountains on the shores of a lake. Several Buddhist monasteries are dotted about the shores, and we went to see them the following day. The buildings containing the cells for the monks are grouped round a court of modest dimensions. We went into one of these cells, which happened to be empty. Its sole furniture was a table with a water pitcher and a miserable couch. We were not allowed to see the other cells, their inmates being busily engaged in study we were told. As it was noon and exceedingly hot, they were no doubt dozing gently over their palm-leaf manuscripts. The so-called studies of the monks chiefly consist in copying manuscripts, the writing being done on strips of palm-leaf. The round letters are quickly pricked into the leaf with a needle held in the right hand, and rested on the thumb-nail of the left hand; the pricked characters being afterwards made legible by being rubbed with black. Such manuscripts are exceedingly cheap; for a couple of rupees I bought a whole bundle of written palm leaves from a hawker in the street, and delighted many a Buddha enthusiast in Europe with a present of one.

Towards evening we went to see the famous Buddha Temple, mixing with the crowd of worshippers that were coming and going. A young monk, seeing that we were strangers, attached himself to us and began drawing our attention to the various objects of interest in the Temple. I had no objections to his doing so, but I was not a little surprised afterwards to find him ask me for a tip when he had finished. "I thought you Buddhists were not allowed to accept money," I said. "I do not want it for myself," was his answer, "but for my books." Buddhism would appear to have lost almost all its ancient severity, though I will not vouch for the truth of a story our guide told me of a monk, who had been put to death for having murdered a rival in a love-affair in which he was engaged.

In the afternoon we drove to Peradeniya to see the famous Botanical Gardens. Thanks to a letter from Freudenberg we were most politely received and shown over the gardens The plain of Colombo proves too hot for many plants, but up here everything is found growing in the open air, coffee, sugar, vanilla, camphor, cocoa, cinnamon, and all sorts of spices dear to us in the days of our youth. A few sheds afforded some protection against wind and rain, but there are no hot-houses, for what will not grow here in the open air has no chance of growing anywhere, many noble trees were shown us, either growing or as specimens of timber. I noticed ebony amongst others, the innermost pith only of which is black, the outer rings differing very little from those of other woods.

After having had tea with the head of the Botanical Gardens, we gladly accepted his offer to show us a tea-plantation. We took a walk between the rows of low tea-bushes, planted at regular intervals from each other, and saw a number of women all busy with creels on their backs. They were picking the leaves singly, the regulation existing that of every seven leaves three may be picked and four must be left on the bush. We now went on to the house, standing in the plantation. The wages were just being paid in one of the rooms. The women were crowding in with their baskets; a boy placed each basket on the scales, and a young Englishman noted the number indicated, and then threw a few coppers from a pile before him to each picker. It was the work of a second, and a great many were disposed of in a very short time, some getting no money, but having their baskets returned with the leaves. All this was done in perfect silence. We also saw the machines for rolling and drying the leaves. Twenty-four hours after the leaves have been picked they are ready for infusing.

We returned to Kandy in a storm of thunder and lightning and rain, no infrequent occurrence in Ceylon. Next morning we went for a walk along the wooded hills of the surroundings before saying good-bye. While walking up from the lake we passed a bread-fruit tree, the unwieldy fruit of which is about the size and shape of a black loaf. It consists of a spongy pulp, in which there are a large number of pips, and it is these pips which people eat and for which the fruit is prized. Prettily laid-out paths lead uphill with charming glimpses of the sea and the town at intervals. These paths are all called after English ladies; Lady Norton's Path, for instance. The sun was still low on the firmament, its rays glittering horizontally through the leaves of the trees; we breathed the lovely fresh morning air, the birds sang, the insects hummed, we were under the spell of the tropical forest. Chatting pleasantly we were walking along a leaf-strewn path, when I luckily noticed that my wife was just on the point of stepping on a black snake that was crawling across our path. Uttering an exclamation of horror I seized and pulled her back; I had got a fright and so had she, and so had the snake, which swiftly glided into the bushes. This was the only snake we chanced to meet with wild, in the whole course of our trip from November to March. Europeans equipped with strong foot-gear, and who have leisure to pick and choose their path, run very little danger in meeting a snake. It is very different for the natives, who work in the fields or wander about after dark with bare legs and feet. They run every danger of stepping on a snake by accident, and who can wonder if the snake retorts with a bite?

Two hours later we were at the station and in one of the streets close by witnessed a scene of which we had often heard. Three Buddhist monks with shaven heads, clothed in long yellow robes, were holding out begging bowls partially concealed by their upper garments. They went from house to house, stopping in front of each door, where they stood in silence till some one came out to lay viands of some description in the bowl. Then they moved on—I need scarcely remind my readers that a Buddhist monk's food has all to be begged for—what the monks manage to collect in the course of a morning on their house to house rounds they partake of at twelve o'clock in their monasteries, and after noon has passed they are not allowed to touch any solid food for the rest of the day. Judging by what I managed to notice, a Buddhist monk's lot seems to be less enviable than a Christian monk's, which is saying a good deal.

On our journey back to Colombo I greatly enjoyed the magnificent scenery, and came to the conclusion that the scenery in Ceylon is far finer than that of India, but that the Singalese are not nearly so interesting as the. Indians. The Buddhism prevailing in Ceylon is characterized not only by a great tolerance, but by an equally great indifference. Neither religious nor political fanatism is to be met with among the Singalese, in consequence perhaps of the island's being an English Colony, and not like India, entirely subject to their foreign masters. In judging of Buddhism in Ceylon, however, I must concur with my friend Garbe in looking upon this religion of love and charity as one of idleness and ignorance.

Nor was this unfavourable impression dispelled by a visit I paid with my friend Freudenberg before leaving Ceylon, to Sumangala, the head of the Buddhist faith in the island. He was a pleasant, little, old man, small in stature, but full of dignity, with a beautiful expression on his face. He spoke fair Sanscrit, and our interview went off very well, but there was none of the fire and enthusiasm I had been wont to meet with in India. The monks present took no part in the conversation, their knowledge of Sanscrit being probably too limited, as was proved later on, when, at a sign from the high priest, the manuscripts, that were in readiness upon tables were shown me. We had some difficulty in arriving at an understanding in a mixture of Sanscrit and Pali.

The 16th of March came ever nearer, the date on which we were to go on board the *Britannia*, touching at Colombo on her voyage home from Australia. It was not without a feeling of regret that I saw myself on the point of bidding farewell to India, though I must say that I was looking forward to my return too. I was anxious to take up my regular work again, and, filled as my mind was with the many impressions and experiences the winter had brought, I longed for a period of peace and rest in which to ponder over and order them. Add to this that about the middle of March the sun is almost straight above Ceylon! At noon one's shadow was a mere patch at one's feet and, one could almost believe one's self to be sharing Peter Schlemihl's fate. Freudenberg gave a splendid dinner party two days before we left, which necessitated my donning evening dress, and in the course of the evening I was most painfully reminded of the difference between the temperature in Ceylon and in Germany. I paid off my servant Purân, giving him ample funds for his return to Cawnpore, and bade him depart in peace, his services being superfluous in a house like Freudenberg's where there were such hosts of servants. Remembering how little fruit is supplied on boardship I gave one of the servants three rupees with instructions to invest it in fruit. He came back with a huge basket full of pine-apples, mangoes, bananas and oranges. But we were not long to enjoy the luxury of fresh fruit. Though we had the fruit taken down to the Freezing-room as soon as we got on board, and only had it taken out at the repasts, signs of decay rapidly set in. We at once gave up the idea of being able to take our supply as far as Aden, and made haste to hand it round the table, to the delight of the other passengers.

CHAPTER IX.

Homeward Bound.

WARNED by our experiences on the *Himalaya* we had been careful to make other and better arrangements about cabins for the voyage home. In Bombay, we had asked to have an upper-deck cabin reserved on the *Britannia,* advertised to sail from Colombo on March 16th, and the agents had taken the order. In the Colombo office, however, the agents declared that they knew nothing of this order, and they could only give us one of the better-class cabins as far as Aden, from which place it was reserved for passengers joining the ship there. Early on Thursday the leviathan could be seen approaching Ceylon—we lunched together for the last time, bade Freudenberg a warm and grateful farewell, and were then rowed in the German Consular boat, manned by twelve swarthy blue-jackets, to the *Britannia.* This created quite a little sensation, which was heightened by the well-pleased faces the sailors wore after I had tipped them. We weighed anchor, and sat rather wistfully watching the lovely landscape gradually disappear in the evening twilight.

The *Britannia* was not so new a vessel as the *Himalaya,* but she was a good sea-going boat. Her Captain was a conscientious, sturdy fellow, with a kind word for each and all of his passengers. The crew did their duty, and the stewards were less lazy than the *Himalaya* ones had been. The passengers too were unlike the boisterous, pleasure-seeking, young people we had travelled out with. Our present shipmates were mostly on their way home from Australia, and were for the greater part staid, elderly people, returning home to retire. Two liberal-minded clergymen, and a doctor, Mr X., with his charming daughter, already formed a little group, with whom we became more closely acquainted. Four young Indians completed our little party, a last echo of our Indian life.

There were two services every Sunday, and we went to hear the hearty, practical sermons preached by the afore-mentioned clergymen. There was no talk of dogma in these sermons; every-day life with its cares and aspirations was their theme, with a quiet but impressive reminder of eternity and the invisible world. "Many people," said one of the clergymen, "have a way of lamenting and grumbling at everything. They live in a bad neighbourhood, in Grumbling Street in fact. We want to pursuade them to come over and live with us in Thanksgiving Street, and take what Providence sends them in a proper spirit."

The following Sunday it was a Missionary who preached, and though I had been advised not to go, I went to hear him preach. I cannot say I was in any way edified.

Our screw had been hard at work day and night for a week after leaving Colombo, when we anchored before Aden on March 23rd, a Thursday. We had to ship the mails from Bombay here, and, as they were not expected to arrive before evening, we had time to go on shore and look about us. At the port itself there are only the harbour buildings and one miserable hotel. The little town of Aden lies at about an hour's distance on the other side of a high mountain ridge. The surroundings are about as forlorn as any landscape the imagination can picture. Not a tree, not a bush, not even a blade of grass, nothing but the sunburnt, arid desert. Rain is said to fall but once every three years —the water is then collected in a system of funnel-shaped cisterns, at the bottom of which we could see a miserable puddle. Close to these cisterns is the "Park of Aden," a bare space, sparsely planted with tiny trees, the dusty half-withered leaves of which drooped disconsolately. These miserable gardens are all that Aden has to boast of in the way of vegetation. We landed in front of the dirty hotel where the traffic was busiest. Jewish money-changers in long caftans, with long curls at their temples, were walking up and down clinking their money. I changed a rupee, though quite prepared for the possibility of being cheated, and so it turned out; I got a bad piece of money in my change, but noticed it too late. I hired a miserable carriage to drive up to the top of the pass, on the other side of which Aden and the cisterns are situated. The coachman, an impertinent Arab, most insolent in bearing, kept objecting to the road I had indicated. I should gladly have got out of the carriage if I could have got another. At last we got to Aden, and rattled along the deserted streets to the market, with its pillared halls. Here I bought a little fruit, but it did not prove to be very good. Everywhere we saw hungry Arab faces on the look-out for an occasion to plunder the strangers, as in Egypt and Palestine. We drove back over the ridge to the harbour, and I was glad to get rid of the rebellious coachman. We then sat down for a little in the crowded hotel, but neither the food nor the beverages looked tempting, so we rowed back to the ship about noon, very glad to be able to take refuge from such an uncivilised, dangerous, and squalid vicinity on board the comfortable steamer. Towards evening the Bombay mail came in, and several hours were spent in transferring the bags and packages from one vessel to the other. It was not nearly so hot on our three days' sail through the Red Sea, as it had been on the voyage out. Early in the morning I woke and found to my surprise our engines had stopped. We are probably letting another steamer past I thought, and hastened on deck to find that our big *Britannia* had run her bows aground, and that the stern was being drifted across to the opposite shore by the current. In front and behind us there were a number of ships whose course we had effectually blocked. On deck the whole crew was feverishly at work, and the Captain, quite red in the face, was hurrying hither and thither, raining orders. I met the English clergyman, who remarked, as he pointed to our situation, "*Britannia* bars the Suez Canal," to which I only retorted "Pull her off." The cause of the mishap was soon explained. The French pilot every steamer is obliged to take on board, had given orders to slow down. The Captain had objected, pointing out that the big vessel would refuse to answer her helm. The pilot had insisted, with the result that we had run aground. The situation threatened to become very unpleasant, for it is one of the regulations that, if a ship fails to get off within four hours, she has to unload, and we knew from the shipping of the Bombay mails what that meant. Meantime, Captain and crew were hard at work, trying to get her off. Strong iron cables were laid across from the bow and stern of the vessel to either shore of canal, where they were fastened to piles. The cables were then drawn taut by the engines, and in this way the monster was gradually made to lie straight, and we could continue our voyage a couple of hours later. It was a magnificent morning; the pure desert air and the north wind were refreshingly cool, and I had the good luck to witness a Fata Morgana, the first I had ever seen. At first, the impression was one of a country road, bordered by rows of acacia trees: a little later it looked as if rows of pelicans were sitting motionless in the distance, and at last the desert appeared to be covered with a stormy lake, above which hovered a town with tall houses and towers and a medley of streets that met and crossed. The illusion was complete and an opera-glass only heightened the reality of the picture; the only unnatural part of it being the way in which the town seemed to float above the water. It lasted for quite an hour too, so we had plenty of leisure to contemplate it.

About mid-day we got to Port Said, where we stopped for a few hours, so I went into the town with our four Indian protégés, to give them a glimpse of Egypt. Towards evening we steamed out of Port

Said, and now the smooth surface of the Indian Ocean and the Red Sea was exchanged for the more animated Mediterranean, which occasionally even threatened to be rough, with dire effects on the passengers, some of whom disappeared altogether. Here and there a female figure was seen reclining like a drooping lily in a deck-chair, and the empty places at table were conspicuous. The following night we passed Crete, and the next morning were off the southern point of Peloponesia, and could view the whole of the lofty snow-covered Taggetos between Sparta and Messema. All day long we steamed northward, passing one Greek island after another, though at a respectful distance. "I used to sail in between the islands," the Captain told me, "but there is no saying what changes the recent earthquake may have caused, so I prefer to keep to the open sea!" Evening came. and good-byes began to be said, for a goodly number of us wanted to land at Brindisi at 3 A. M. Very few thought of trying to snatch a few hours' sleep, so great was the prevailing confusion. At 1 A. M. a substantial English breakfast was served, and soon after two o'clock we took leave of our good ship, landing, not in boats as we had hitherto done, but pacing proudly across the gangway on to the pier which the English Company has had built here on Italian soil. We got to Naples the same day, where dear friends were waiting to welcome us. After a few days' stay in Naples we went on to Rome, and hastened home *via* Milan, Bâla and Mayence, arriving safe and sound about the middle of April.

APPENDIX A.

THE PHILOSOPHY OF THE VEDANTA.*

BY DR. PAUL DEUSSEN.

[*Professor of Philosophy in the University of Kiel, Germany.*]

On my journey through India I have noticed with satisfaction that in philosophy till now our brothers in the East have maintained a very good tradition, better perhaps, than the more active but less contemplative branches of the great Indo-Aryan family in Europe, where Empiricism, Realism and their natural consequence, Materialism, grow from day to day more exuberantly, whilst metaphysics, the very centre and heart of serious philosophy, are supported only by a few ones who have learned to brave the spirit of the age.

In India, the influence of this perverted and perversive spirit of our age has not yet overthrown in religion and philosophy the good traditions of the great ancient time. It is true, that most of the ancient *darsanas* even in India find only an historical interest; followers of the Sankhya-System occur rarely; Nyaya is cultivated mostly as an intellectual sport and exercise, like grammar or mathematics,—but the Vedântic is, now as in the ancient time, living in the mind and heart of every thoughtful Hindu. It is true, that even here in the sanctuary of Vedântic metaphysics, the realistic tendencies, natural to man, have penetrated, producing the misinterpreting variations of Sankara's Adwyaita, known under the names Visishtâdvaita, Dwyaita, Suddhâdwyaita of Râmânuja, Mâdhva, Vallabha,—but India till now has not yet been seduced by their voices, and of hundred Vedântins (I have it from a well-informed man, who is himself a zealous adversary of Sankara and follower of Râmânuja) fifteen perhaps adhere to Râmânuja, five Mâdhva, five to Vallabha, and seventy-five to Sankaracharya

This fact may be for poor India in so many misfortunes a great consolation; for the eternal interests are higher than the temporary ones; and the system of the Vedânta, as founded on the Upanishads and Vedânta Sutras and accomplished by Sankara's commentaries on them,—equal in rank to Plato and Kant—is one of the most valuable products of the genius of mankind in his researches of the eternal truth,—as I propose to show now by a short sketch of Sankara's Adwyaita and comparison of its principal doctrines with the best that Occidental philosophy has produced till now.

---

* An address, delivered before the Bombay Branch of the Royal Asiatic Society, Saturday, the 25th February, 1893.

Taking the Upanishads, as Sankara does, for revealed truth with absolute authority, it was not an easy task to build out of their materials a consistent philosophical system, for the Upanishads are in Theology, Cosmology and Psychology full of the hardest contradictions. So in many passages the nature of Brahman is painted out in various and luxuriant colours, and again we read, that the nature of Brahman is quite unattainable to human words, to human understanding;—so we meet sometimes longer reports explaining how the world has been created by Brahman, and again we are told, that there is no world besides Brahman, and all variety of things is mere error and illusion;—so we have fanciful descriptions of the Samsara, the way of the wandering soul up the heaven and back to the earth, and again read that there is no Samsara, no variety of souls at all, but only one Atman, who is fully and totally residing in every being.

Sankara in these difficulties created by the nature of his materials, in face of so many contradictory doctrines, which he was not allowed to decline and yet could not admit altogether,—has found a wonderful way out, which deserves the attention, perhaps the imitation of the Christian dogmatists in their embarrassments. He constructs out of the materials of the Upanishads two systems: one esoteric, philosophical (called by him *nirguna vidya* sometimes *paramarthika avastha*) containing the metaphysical truth for the few ones, rare in all times and countries, who are able to understand it; and another exoteric, Theological (*saguna vidya, vyavhariki avastha*) for the general public, who want images, not abstract truth, worship, not meditation.

I shall now point out briefly the two systems esoteric and exoteric, in pursuing and confronting them through the four chief parts, which Sankara's system contains, and every complete philosophical system must contain:—

I. Theology, the doctrine of God or of the philosophical principle.

II. Cosmology, the doctrine of the world.

III. Psychology, the doctrine of the soul.

IV. Eschatology, the doctrine of the last things, the things after death.

I.—THEOLOGY.

The Upanishads swarm with fanciful and contradictory descriptions of the nature of Brahman. He is the all-pervading akasa, is the purusha in the sun, the purusha in the eye: his head is the heaven, his eyes are sun and moon, his breath is the wind, his footstool the earth; he is infinitely great as soul of the universe and infinitely small as the soul in us; he is in particular the *Isvara*, the personal God, distributing justly reward and punishment according to the deeds of man. All these numerous descriptions are collected by Sankara under the wide mantle of the exoteric theololgy, the *saguna vidya* of Brahman, consisting of numerous "vidyas" adapted for approaching the

Eternal Being not by the way of knowledge but by the way of worshipping, and having each its particular fruits. Mark, that also the conception of God as a personal being, an *Isvara*, is merely exoteric and does not give us a conform knowledge of the Atman;—and, indeed, when we consider what is personality, how narrow in its limitations, how closely connected to egoism the counterpart of Godly essence, who might think so low of God, to impute him personality?

In the sharpest contrast to these exoteric vidyas stands the esoteric, *nirguna vidya* of the Atman; and its fundamental tenet is the absolute inaccessibility of God to human thoughts and words:

यतो वाचो निवर्तन्ते

अप्राप्य मनसा सह.

and again:

अविज्ञातं विजानताम्

विज्ञातमविजानताम्.

and the celebrated formula occurring so often in Brihadâranyaka-Upanishad; *neti! neti*, *viz*., whatever attempt you make to know the Atman, whatever description you give of him, I always say: *na iti, na iti*, it is not so, it is not so! Therefore, the wise Bhava, when asked by the king Vâshkalin, to explain, the Brahman kept silence. And when the king repeated his request again and again, the Rishi broke out into the answer: "I tell it you, but you don't understand it; *canto yam atma*, this Atma is silence!" We know it now by the Kantian philosophy, that the answer of Bhava was correct, we know it that the very organisation of our intellect (which is bound once for ever to its innate forms of intuition, space, time, and causality) excludes us from a knowledge of the spaceless, timeless, Godly reality for ever and ever. And yet the Atman, the only Godly being is not unattainable to us, is even not far from us, for, we have it fully and totally in ourselves as our own metaphysical entity; and here when returning from the outside and apparent world to the deepest secrets of our own nature, we may come to God, not by knowledge, but by *anubhava*, by absorption into our own self. There is a great difference between knowledge, in which subject and object are distinct from each other, and *anubhava* where subject and object coincide in the same. He who by *anubhava* comes to the great intelligence, "*aham brahma asmi*," obtains a state called by Sankara *Samradhanam*, accomplished satisfaction; and indeed, what might he desire, who feels and vows himself as the sum and totality of all existence!

II.—COSMOLOGY.

Here again we meet the distinction of exoteric and esoteric doctrine, though not so clearly severed by Sankara as in other parts of his system.

The exoteric Cosmology according to the natural but erroneous realism (*avidya*) in which we are born, considers this world as the reality and can express its entire dependency of Brahman only by the mythical way of a creation of the world, by Brahman. So a temporal creation of the world, even as in the Christian documents, is also taught in various and well-known passages of the Upanishads But such a creation of the material world by an immaterial cause, performed in a certain point of time after an eternity elapsed uselessly, is not only against the demands of human reason and natural science, but also against another important doctrine of the Vedânta, which teaches and must teach (as we shall see hereafter) the "beginninglessness of the migration of souls," *samsarasya anaditvam*. Here the expedient of Sankara is very clever and worthy of imitation. Instead of the temporary creation once for ever of the Upanishads, he teaches that the world in great periods is created and reabsorbed by Brahman (referring to the misunderstood verse of the Rig Veda: सूर्याचन्द्रमसौ धाता यथा पूर्वमकल्पयत् this mutual creation and reabsorption lasts from eternity) and no creation can be allowed by our system to be a first one, and that for good reasons, as we shall see just now. If we ask: *Why* has God created the world? The answers to this question are generally very unsatisfactory. For his own glorification? How may we attribute to him so much vanity!—For his particular amusement? But he was an eternity without this play-toy!—By love of mankind? How may he love a thing before it exists; and how may it be called love, to create millions for misery and eternal pain!—The Vedanta has a better answer. The never ceasing new-creation of the world is a moral necessity connected with the central and most valuable doctrine of the exoteric Vedânta, the doctrine of Samsara.

Man, says Sankara, is like a plant. He grows, flourishes and at the end he dies but not totally. For as the plant, when dying. leaves behind it the seed, of which, according to its quality, a new plant grows;—so man, when dying, leaves his *Karma*, the good and bad works of his life, which must be rewarded and punished in another life after this. No life can be the first, for it is the fruit of previous actions, nor the last, for its actions must be expiated in a next following life. So the Samsara is without beginning and without end, and the new creation of the world after every absorption into Brahman is a moral necessity. I need not point out, in particular here in India, the high value of this doctrine of Samsara as a consolation in the distresses, as a moral agent in the temptations of life;—I have to say here only, that the

Samsara, though not the absolute truth, is a mythical representative of truth which in itself is unattainable to our intellect: mythical is this theory of metempsychosis only in so far as it invests in the forms of space and time what really is spaceless and timeless and therefore beyond the reach of our understanding. So the Samsara is just so far from the truth, as the *saguna vidya* is from the *nirguna vidya*; it is the eternal truth itself, but (since we cannot conceive it otherwise) the truth in an allegorical form, adapted to our human understanding. And this is the character of the whole exoteric Vedanta, whilst the esoteric doctrine tries to find out the philosophical, the absolute truth.

And so we come to the esoteric Cosmology, whose simple doctrine is this, that in reality there is no manifold world, but only Brahman, and that what we consider as the world is a mere illusion (*maya*) similar to a *mrigatrishnika*, which disappears when we approach it, and not more to be feared than the rope, which we took in the darkness for a serpent. There are, as you see, many similes in the Vedânta, to illustrate the illusive character of this world, but the best of them is perhaps when Sankara compares our life with a long dream: – a man whilst dreaming does not doubt of the reality of the dream, but this reality disappears in the moment of awakening, to give place to a truer reality, which we were not aware of whilst dreaming. The life a dream! this has been the thought of many wise men from Pindar and Sophocles to Shakspeare and Calderon de la Barca, but nobody has better explained this idea, than Sankara. And, indeed, the moment when we die may be to nothing so similar as to the awakening from a long and heavy dream; it may be, that then heaven and earth are blown away like the nightly phantoms of the dream, and that then may stand before us? or rather in us? Brahman the eternal reality, which was hidden to us till then by this dream of life!—This world is maya, is illusion, is not the very reality, that is the deepest thought of the esoteric Vedanta attained not by calculating *tarka* but by *anubhava*, by returning from this variegated word to the deep recess of our own self (*Atman*). Do so, if you can and you will get aware of a reality very different from empirical reality, a timeless, spaceless, changeless reality, and you will feel and experience that whatever is outside of this only true reality is mere appearance, is maya, is a dream!— This was the way the Indian thinkers went, and by a similar way, shown by Parmenides, Plato came to the same truth, when knowing and teaching that this world is a world of shadows, and that the reality is not in these shadows, but behind them. The accord here of Platonism and Vedantism is wonderful, but both have grasped this great metaphysical truth by intuition; their tenet is true, but they are not able to prove it, and in so far they are defective. And here a great light and assistance to the Indian and the Grecian thinker comes from the philosophy of Kant, who went quite another way, not the Vedântic and Platonic way of intuition, but the way of abstract reasoning and scientific proof. The great work of Kant is an analysis of human mind, not in the superficial way of Locke, but getting to the very bottom of it. And in doing so Kant found, to the surprise of the world and of himself, that three essential elements of this outside world, *viz.*, space, time and causality, are not, as we naturally believe, eternal fundaments of an objective reality, but merely subjective, innate, intuitive forms of our own intellect. This has been proved by Kant and by his great disciple Schopenhauer with mathematical evidence, and I have given these proofs (the fundament of every scientific metaphysics) in the shortest and clearest form in my "Elemete der, Metaphysik"—a book which I am resolved now to get translated into English, for the benefit not of the Europeans (who may learn German) but of my brothers in India, who will be greatly astonished to find in Germany the scientific substruction of their own philosophy, of the Adawyaita Vedânta! For Kant has demonstrated, that space, time and causality are not objective realities, but only subjective forms of our intellect, and the unavoidable conclusion is this, that the world, as far as it is extended in space, running on in time, ruled throughout by causality, in so far is merely a representation of my mind and nothing beyond it. You see the concordance of Indian, Grecian and German metaphysics; the world is maya, is illusion, says Sankara;—it is a world of shadows, not of realities, says *Plato;* —it is "appearance only, not the thing in itself," says *Kant.* Here we have the same doctrine in three different parts of the world, but the scientific proofs of it are not in Sankara, not in Plato, but only in Kant

III.—PSYCHOLOGY.

Here we convert the order and begin with the esoteric Psychology, because it is closely connected with the esoteric cosmology and its fundamental doctrine; the world is *maya*. All is illusive, with one exception, with the exception of my own Self, of my Atman. My Atman cannot be illusive, as Sankara shows, anticipating the "*cogito, ergo sum*" of Descartes,—for he who would deny it, even in denying it, witnesses its reality. But what is the relation between my individual soul, the Jiva-Atman and the highest soul, the Parama-Atman or Brahman? Here Sankara, like prophet, foresees the deviations of Ramanuja, Madhva and Vallabha and refutes them in showing, that the Jiva cannot be a part of Brahman (Ramanuja), because Brahman is without parts (for it is timeless and spaceless, and all parts are either successions in time or co-ordinations in space,—as we may supply),—neither a different thing from Brahman (Madhva), for Brahman is *ekam eva advitiyam*, as we may experience by *anubhava*, —nor a metamorphose of Brahman (Vallabha), for Brahman is unchangeable (for, as we know by Kant, it is out of causality). The conclusion is, that the Jiva, being neither a part nor a different thing, nor a variation of Brahman, must be the Paramatman fully and totally himself, a conclusion made equally by the Vedanta in Sankara, by the Platonic Plotinos and by the Kantian Schopenhaure. But Sankara in his conclusions goes perhaps further than any of them. If really our soul, says he, is not a part of Brahman all-pervadingness, eternity, all-mightiness (scientifically spoken: exemption of space, time, causality) are ours; *aham brahama asmi*, I am Brahman, and consequently I am all-pervading (spaceless) eternal (timeless,) almighty (not limited in my doing by causality). But these godly qualities are hidden in me, says Sankara, as the fire is hidden in the wood and will appear only after the final deliverance.

What is the cause of this concealment of my godly nature? The Upadhis, answers Sankara, and with this answer we pass from the esoteric to the exoteric psychology. The Upadhis are manas and indriyas, prana with its five branches, sukshman sariram,—in short, the whole psychological apparatus, which together with a factor changeable from birth to birth, with my karman, accompanies my Atman in all his ways of migration without infecting his godly nature, as the crystal is not infected by the colour painted over it. But wherefrom originate these Upadhis? They form of course part of the *maya*, the great world illusion, and like *maya* they are based in our innate *avidya* or ignorance, a merely negative power and yet strong enough to keep us from our godly existence. But now, from where comes the *avidya*, this primeval cause of ignorance, sin, and misery? Here all philosophers in India and Greece and everywhere have been defective, until Kant came to show us that the whole question is inadmissible. You ask for the cause of *avidya*, but she has no cause; for causality goes only so far as this world of the Samsara goes, connecting each link of it with another, but never beyond Samsara and its fundamental characteristic the *avidya*. In enquiring after a cause of *avidya* with *maya*, Samsara and Upadhis, you abuse, as Kant may teach us, your innate mental organ of causality to penetrate into a region for which it is not made and where it is no more available. The fact is, that we are here in ignorance, sin and misery, and that we know the way out of them, but the question of a cause for them is senseless.

IV.—Eschatology.

And now a few words about this way out of the Samsara, and first about the exoteric theory of it. In the ancient time of the hymns there was no idea of Samsara but only rewards in heaven and (somewhat later) punishment in a dark region (*padam gabhiram*), the precursor of the later hells. Then the deep theory of Samsara came up, teaching reward and punishment in the form of a new birth on earth. The Vedanta combines both theories, and so he has a double expiation, first in heaven and hell, and then again in a new existence on the earth. This double expiation is different (1) for performers of good works, going the *Pitriyana*, (2) for worshippers of the Sagunam Brahma, going the *Devyana*, (3) for wicked deeds, leading to what is obscurely hinted at in the Upanishads as the *Tritiyam Sthanam*, the third place—(1) the *Pitriyana* leads through a succession of dark spheres to the moon, there to enjoy the fruit of the good works and, after their consumption, back to an earthly existence; (2) the *Devayana* leads through a set of brighter spheres to Brahman, without returning to the earth (तेषां न पुनरावृत्तिः). But this Brahman is only Sagunam Brahma, the object of worshipping, and its true worshippers, though entering into this Sagunam Brahma without returning, have to wait in it until they get *moksha* by obtaining *samayogadarshanam*, the full knowledge of the Nirgunam Brahma. (3) The *Tritiyam Sthanam* including the later theories of hells, teaches punishment in them, and again punishment by returning to earth in the form of lower castes, animals and plant. All these various and fantastical ways of Samsara are considered as true, quite as true as this world is, but not more. For the whole and the whole way of Samsara is valid and true for those only who are in the *avidya*, not for those who have overcome her, as we have to show now.

The esoteric Vedânta does not admit the reality of the world nor of the Samsara, for the only reality is Brahman, seized in ourselves as our own Atman. The Knowledge of this Atman, the great intelligence: "*aham brahma asmi*," does not produce *moksha* (deliverance), but is *moksha* itself. Then we obtain what the Upanishads say:

भिद्यते हृदयग्न्धिः
छिद्यन्ते सर्वशंशयाः ।
क्षीयन्ते चास्य कर्याणि
तस्मिन्दृष्टे परावेर ।

When seeing Brahma as the highest and the lowest everywhere, all knots of our heart, all sorrows are split, all doubts vanish, and our works become nothing. Certainly, no man can live without doing works, and so also the *Jivanmukta*; but he knows it, that all these works are illusive, as the whole world is, and therefore they do not adhere to him nor produce for him a new life after death—And what kind of works may such a man do?—People have often reproached the Vedânta with being defective in morals and, indeed, the Indian genius is too contemplative to speak much of works; but the fact is nevertheless, that the highest and purest morality is the immediate consequence of the Vedânta. The Gospels fix quite correctly as the highest law of morality: "love your neighbour as yourselves." But why should I do so, since by the order of nature I feel pain and pleasure only in myself, not in my neighbour? The answer is not in the Bible (this venerable book being not yet quite free of Semetic realism), but it is in the Veda, is in the great formula "*tat tvam asi*," which gives in three words metaphysics and morals altogether. You shall love your neighbour as yourselves,—because you are your neighbour, and mere illusion makes you believe, that your neighbour is something different from yourselves. Or in the words of the Bhagavad-Gita: he, who knows himself in everything and everything in himself, will not injure himself by himself, *Nahinasti almana atmanam.* This is the sum and tenor of all morality, and this is the standpoint of a man knowing himself as Branman. He feels himself as everything—so he will not desire anything, for he has whatever can be had;—he feels himself as everything—so he will not injure anything, for nobody injures himself. He lives in the world, is surrounded by its illusions but not deceived by them: like the man suffering from *timira*, who sees two moons but knows that there is one only, so the Jivanmukta sees the manifold world and cannot get rid of seeing it, but he knows, that there is only one being, Brahman, the Atman, his own Self, and he verifies it by his deeds of pure uninterested morality. And so he expects his end, like the potter expects the end of the twirling of his wheel, after the vessel is ready. And then, for him, when death comes, no more Samsara: न तस्य प्राणा उत्क्रामन्ति । ब्रह्म एव सन् ब्रह्म अप्येति! He enters into Brahman, like the streams into the ocean: he leaves behind him *nama* and *rupam*, he leaves behind him

यथा नद्यः स्यन्दमानाः समुद्रे
अस्तं गच्छन्ति नामरूपे विहाय
तथा विद्वान् नामरूपाद्विमुक्तः
परात्परं पुरुषमुपैति दिव्यम्

individuality, but he does not leave behind him his *Atmana*, his self. It is not the falling of the drop into the infinite ocean, it is the whole ocean, becoming free from the fetters of ice, returning from his frozen state to what he is really and has never ceased to be, to his own all-pervading, eternal, all mighty nature. And so the Vedânta, in its unfalsified form, is the strongest support of pure morality, is the greatest consolation in the sufferings of life and death,—Indians, keep to it!—

Biographies of Eminent Indians

A Series of Uniform Booklets each with a Portrait

Foolscap 8vo. Price As. Four each

The aim of this Series is to present within a short compass sketches of the lives and careers of all eminent Indians. Each Volume besides giving a succinct biographical sketch contains copious extracts from the speeches and writings of the personages described. The Series has been pronounced by the Press to be "the most welcome addition to Indian, biographical and critical literature."

Dadabhai Naoroji	K. T. Telang
Sir P. M. Mehta	Surendranath Banerjea
Dinsha Edulji Wacha	Romesh Chunder Dutt
Mahadev Govind Ranade	Ananda Mohan Bose
Sri Ramakrishna Paramahamsa	W. C. Bonnerjee
	Budruddin Tyabji
Swami Vivekananda	Sir Syed Ahmed
Hon. Mr. G. K. Gokhale	*Lal Mohun Ghose*
Dr. Rash Behari Ghose	M. K. Gandhi
Lala Lajpat Rai	Madan Mohan Malaviya
Ravi Varma	Babu Kristo Das Pal
Toru Dutt	R. N. Mudholkar

Price As. 4 Each. 1 Doz. at a time As. 3 each.

G. A. Natesan & Co., Sunkurama Chetty Street, Madras.

THE SANJ VARTMAN. Messrs. Natesan & Co. are doing a distinct and national service by issuing brief sketches of the lives of men who have played an important part in the modern epochs of Indian history.

THE INDU PRAKASH. It goes without saying that the lives are well written and the usefulness of the brochures is enhanced by copious extracts from the speeches and writings of the subjects of the portraits.

A:

Shakespeare's Chart of Life

BEING STUDIES OF

HAMLET, KING LEAR, OTHELLO AND MACBETH

BY THE REV. DR. WILLIAM MILLER, C.I.E.

CONTENTS.

KING LEAR AND INDIAN POLITICS
HAMLET AND THE WASTE OF LIFE
MACBETH AND THE RUIN OF SOULS
OTHELLO AND THE CRASH OF CHARACTER

Dr. Miller does not appear as an annotator or critic. He fixes his student's attention especially on the ethical side of Shakespeare's teaching. According to him the plays of Shakespeare, whether designedly or not, are not calculated merely to amuse. They have each "an inner meaning," a "central idea," which it does the student good to search out and assimilate.

The Madras Mail.—Dr. Miller has taught Shakespeare for over 40 years to hundreds of students, who have passed through the Christian College. And in his classes, if he has enforced one lesson more than another, it has been that these plays must have been written with the object, among others, of making plain the moral principles, which underlie the ordinary occurrences in human life, and that it is this feature of Shakespeare's plays which makes them not only an intellectual discipline but a means of real benefit to those upon whom they have their full and proper influence.

Rs. 4. To Subscribers of the "Indian Review," Rs. 3.

Available Separately Re. One each.

G. A. Natesan & Co., Sunkurama Chetty Street, Madras.

THE VOICE OF INDIA.—We have no doubt that, after perusing the main outlines of Dr. Miller's criticism of these four great tragedies of Shakespeare's, the reader's interest will be roused for the books themselves.

THE HINDU.—* * Every Indian and every European should carefully read through and think over the wise observations with which the book is replete.

THE CIVIL AND MILITARY GAZETTE:—Dr. Miller's book is full of suggestive thought.

G. A. Natesan & Co.'s Publications.

The Guzerati :—Many of our countrymen are deeply indebted to the head of the enterprising firm of G. A. Natesan & Co., Madras, for the valuable publications they have been placing before the Indian public dealing with important questions of contemporary interest or with the lives and careers of some of our foremost Indians, both ancient and modern. We do not think there is any other publishing house in India that has attempted what Mr. Natesan has done with so much success during the last four years to instruct public opinion by means of handy, cheap and useful publications. Mr. Natesan is not only a man of literary attainments but endowed with business capacity and sound discernment. He certainly deserves to be congratulated on the success of his useful publications.

The Sanjvartman :—There are certainly no publishing houses in India that can at all be compared with those of Murray, Constable, Blackie and Macmillan in England. Such historic concerns apart, there are very few firms that take the trouble of being up-to-date, or by the variety of their publications to form and direct the public taste or to diffuse useful and interesting knowledge among their constituents. Among these few Messrs. Natesan and Company of Madras undoubtedly occupy the place of honour. The *Indian Review*, published by Mr. Natesan, is undoubtedly a gem of its kind and no cultured Indian cares to be without it. But the Review represents only one side of Mr. Natesan's activity. Not a month elapses but this enterprising firm brings out elaborate volumes on every kind of subject that affects the interests of India and they are generally the work of men who know what they are writing about. But one of the most popular outputs of the firm is the string of short, succinct and instructive biographies of eminent Indians which are published from day to day * * * Messrs. Natesan & Co., are doing a distinct and national service by issuing brief sketches of the lives of men who have played an important part in the modern epochs of Indian History. We thankfully acknowledge the receipt of all these and have great pleasure in briefly noticing them.

THE IMPROVEMENT OF

INDIAN AGRICULTURE

SOME LESSONS FROM AMERICA

By Mrs. Saint Nihal Singh

AUTHOR OF

"*The House Hygienic*" "*My Favourite Recipes*"
"*How to Make Good Things to Eat*"
"*The Virtues of Varnish,*" etc.

TABLE OF CONTENTS

Crown 8vo, 160 pages

Price Re. 1. To Subscribers, As. 12.
